Anti-Inflammatory Diet

for Arthritis

Dr. Madison Wells

Table of Content

Introduction

As a physician who has dedicated my career to helping individuals manage chronic conditions, I have witnessed firsthand the profound impact that lifestyle changes can have on one's health and well-being. This is particularly true for those living with arthritis, a condition that affects millions of people worldwide and can significantly impact their quality of life.

The idea for this book was born out of a conversation with my dear friend, Emily, who had been struggling with rheumatoid arthritis for years. Despite trying various medications and treatments, she found herself in constant pain and feeling hopeless. Over a cup of tea, we discussed the potential benefits of adopting an anti-inflammatory diet and lifestyle. Emily was intrigued but overwhelmed, unsure of where to start or how to make sustainable changes.

Inspired by Emily's story and the countless others I have encountered in my practice, I set out to create a comprehensive guide that would empower individuals with arthritis to take control of their health through nutrition and lifestyle modifications. This book is the result of years of research, clinical experience, and collaboration with experts in the field of rheumatology and integrative medicine.

Inside, you will find a wealth of information and practical tools to help you adopt an anti-inflammatory diet and lifestyle, including:

- A clear explanation of the science behind inflammation and its role in arthritis
- Detailed guidance on which foods to eat and avoid to reduce inflammation and manage symptoms
- Delicious, easy-to-prepare recipes suitable for various dietary preferences and restrictions
- A 14-day meal plan with a complete shopping list to help you get started
- Practical tips for making sustainable lifestyle changes, such as stress management techniques and exercise recommendations
- Real-life success stories from individuals who have transformed their health and well-being through an anti-inflammatory approach

Whether you are newly diagnosed with arthritis or have been living with the condition for years, this book offers a holistic, evidence-based approach to managing your symptoms and improving your overall health. By providing you with the knowledge, tools, and inspiration needed to make lasting changes, this book aims to empower you on your journey towards a more vibrant, pain-free life.

I am confident that the information and strategies presented in this book can make a meaningful difference in your life, just as they have for Emily and countless others. So, let's embark on this transformative journey together, one page at a time.

This book is dedicated to Emily, whose unwavering spirit in the face of adversity has been a guiding light throughout this project.

Chapter 1: Arthritis 101

1.1 What is arthritis? Types and symptoms

Arthritis is a broad term that encompasses over 100 different conditions affecting the joints, surrounding tissues, and other connective tissues. While arthritis is often associated with older adults, it can impact people of all ages, including children. The two most common forms of arthritis are osteoarthritis (OA) and rheumatoid arthritis (RA), each with its own unique causes and characteristics.

Understanding Osteoarthritis

Osteoarthritis, the most prevalent type of arthritis, is often referred to as "wear and tear" arthritis. This condition occurs when the protective cartilage that cushions the ends of your bones gradually deteriorates over time. As the cartilage wears away, the bones begin to rub against each other, causing pain, stiffness, and inflammation in the affected joints.

OA most commonly affects the joints in the hands, knees, hips, and spine. The symptoms of osteoarthritis tend to develop slowly and worsen over time. You may experience pain during movement, tenderness when applying pressure to the joint, stiffness after periods of inactivity, and a grating sensation or popping sound when the joint is in motion.

In advanced stages of OA, the joint pain may become constant, making it difficult to perform everyday tasks like walking, climbing stairs, or opening jars. The affected joints may also appear swollen and develop bony spurs or lumps, known as osteophytes.

Defining Rheumatoid Arthritis

Rheumatoid arthritis is an autoimmune disorder in which the body's immune system mistakenly attacks the lining of the joints, called the synovium. This attack causes inflammation, swelling, and pain in the affected joints. Over time, the persistent inflammation can lead to joint deformity and erosion of the bones.

Unlike osteoarthritis, RA typically affects the joints symmetrically, meaning that if one hand or knee is affected, the other is likely to be as well. The most commonly affected joints include the hands, wrists, feet, ankles, knees, and shoulders.

Symptoms of rheumatoid arthritis often include joint pain, stiffness (especially in the morning or after periods of inactivity), swelling, warmth, and redness in the affected joints. Fatigue, low-grade fever, and a general feeling of being unwell are also common.

RA can also cause inflammation in other parts of the body, such as the eyes, lungs, heart, and blood vessels. This systemic inflammation can lead to additional health complications beyond joint damage.

Less Common Forms of Arthritis

While osteoarthritis and rheumatoid arthritis are the most well-known types, there are many other forms of arthritis and related conditions, including:

- Psoriatic Arthritis: An inflammatory joint condition that often occurs alongside the skin condition psoriasis.
- Gout: A painful form of arthritis caused by the buildup of uric acid crystals in the joints, most often affecting the big toe.
- Lupus: An autoimmune disorder that can cause inflammation and pain in the joints, skin, and other organs.
- Ankylosing Spondylitis: A type of arthritis that primarily affects the spine, causing inflammation and stiffness in the vertebrae.
- Juvenile Arthritis: A group of conditions that cause joint inflammation and stiffness in children and teenagers.

Living with Arthritis

Regardless of the type of arthritis you have, living with the condition can be challenging. The pain, stiffness, and reduced mobility can make everyday activities feel like insurmountable obstacles. You may find yourself struggling to get dressed, prepare meals, or even get out of bed in the morning.

The emotional toll of arthritis can be just as significant as the physical symptoms. Feeling frustrated, depressed, or angry about your limitations is common. You may worry about becoming a burden to your loved ones or fear that your condition will only worsen with time.

It's essential to remember that while there is no cure for arthritis, there are many ways to manage your symptoms and improve your quality of life. In the following chapters, we'll explore how an anti-inflammatory diet can be a powerful tool in your arthritis management toolkit, helping to reduce pain, increase mobility, and reclaim your independence.

1.2 Conventional treatments and their limitations

When faced with the pain and limitations of arthritis, it's natural to turn to conventional medical treatments for relief. While these treatments can be helpful in managing symptoms, they often come with their own set of challenges and limitations. Understanding the potential benefits and drawbacks of these conventional approaches can help you make informed decisions about your arthritis management plan.

Medication: A Double-Edged Sword

One of the most common conventional treatments for arthritis is medication. Non-steroidal anti-inflammatory drugs (NSAIDs), such as ibuprofen and naproxen, can help reduce pain and inflammation in the joints. Prescription NSAIDs, like celecoxib, may be recommended for more severe cases. While these medications can provide temporary relief, they also come with the risk of side effects, including stomach irritation, ulcers, and even an increased risk of heart attack or stroke when used long-term.

For those with rheumatoid arthritis, disease-modifying antirheumatic drugs (DMARDs) may be prescribed to slow down joint damage and prevent the condition from worsening. These medications, such as methotrexate and sulfasalazine, work by suppressing the immune system. While they can be effective in managing RA, they also increase the risk of infections and can cause other side effects like nausea, fatigue, and liver damage.

Corticosteroids, another class of medications used to treat arthritis, are powerful anti-inflammatory drugs that can quickly reduce pain and swelling. However, long-term use of corticosteroids can lead to serious side effects, including weight gain, osteoporosis, and an increased risk of diabetes.

The side effects and potential long-term risks associated with arthritis medications can be daunting. Many people find themselves caught in a cycle of trying different drugs, each with its own set of challenges, in search of relief. The prospect of having to rely on these medications indefinitely can be frustrating and disheartening.

The Limits of Physical Therapy and Exercise

Physical therapy and exercise are often recommended as part of an arthritis management plan. Strengthening the muscles around the affected joints and improving flexibility can help reduce pain and stiffness. Low-impact exercises, such as swimming, cycling, and yoga, are often encouraged for people with arthritis.

While these activities can be beneficial, they also have their limitations. For some, the pain and stiffness of arthritis can make even gentle exercises challenging. The fear of exacerbating joint pain can lead to a sedentary lifestyle, which can actually worsen arthritis symptoms over time. Additionally, access to physical therapy and guided exercise programs can be limited by financial constraints or a lack of nearby resources.

Surgery: A Last Resort

In severe cases of arthritis, particularly when the joint damage is extensive, surgery may be recommended. Joint replacement surgery, such as a hip or knee replacement, can help relieve pain and improve mobility. However, these surgeries come with their own set of risks and challenges.

The recovery process from joint replacement surgery can be lengthy and painful. There is a risk of complications, such as infection or blood clots. Even after recovery, the replaced joint may not function as well as a healthy, natural joint. The thought of undergoing surgery and the potential for a difficult recovery can be daunting for many people with arthritis.

The Frustration of Ineffective Treatments

Perhaps one of the most frustrating aspects of conventional arthritis treatments is that what works for one person may not work for another. You may find yourself trying multiple medications, exercises, or therapies without finding the relief you desperately need. The trial-and-error process can be exhausting, both physically and emotionally.

It's not uncommon to feel like you've exhausted all your options when conventional treatments fail to provide adequate relief. The limitations of these approaches can leave you feeling helpless and stuck, wondering if you'll ever find a way to manage your arthritis effectively.

The Search for Alternative Solutions

Recognizing the limitations of conventional arthritis treatments, many people begin to explore alternative approaches to managing their condition. This is where the power of nutrition comes into play. In the following chapters, we'll delve into the role of inflammation in arthritis and how an anti-inflammatory diet can be a game-changer in managing symptoms and improving quality of life.

While conventional treatments certainly have their place in arthritis management, they are not the only option. By understanding the potential benefits and limitations of these approaches, you can make informed decisions about your care and explore complementary strategies, like dietary changes, to take control of your arthritis and reclaim your life.

1.3 The role of inflammation in arthritis

Inflammation: The Body's Double-Edged Sword

Inflammation is a natural and essential part of the body's immune response. When you get a cut or catch a cold, inflammation is the body's way of fighting off harmful invaders and promoting healing. However, when inflammation becomes chronic, it can lead to a host of health problems, including arthritis.

In the case of arthritis, chronic inflammation is at the root of the pain, stiffness, and joint damage that so many people struggle with daily. Understanding the role of inflammation in arthritis is crucial for finding effective ways to manage the condition and improve quality of life.

Osteoarthritis: When Wear and Tear Meets Inflammation

Osteoarthritis, the most common form of arthritis, is often thought of as a "wear and tear" condition. As we age, the cartilage that cushions our joints begins to break down, leading to pain and stiffness. However, recent research has shown that inflammation also plays a significant role in the development and progression of osteoarthritis.

When the cartilage in a joint becomes damaged, it releases substances that trigger an inflammatory response in the body. This inflammation can cause further damage to the cartilage and the surrounding tissues, leading to a vicious cycle of joint deterioration and pain.

Chronic low-grade inflammation in osteoarthritis can also be fueled by factors like obesity, poor diet, and a sedentary lifestyle. Excess body weight puts extra stress on weight-bearing joints, while unhealthy foods and lack of exercise can contribute to systemic inflammation throughout the body.

Rheumatoid Arthritis: When the Immune System Attacks

Rheumatoid arthritis is an autoimmune disease in which the body's immune system mistakenly attacks the lining of the joints, causing inflammation, swelling, and pain. This chronic inflammation can lead to permanent joint damage and deformity if left unchecked.

In RA, the inflammatory process is driven by an overactive immune system that releases a flood of inflammatory chemicals called cytokines. These cytokines, such as tumor necrosis factor (TNF) and interleukin-6 (IL-6), fuel the inflammatory fires and contribute to the destruction of cartilage and bone.

The exact cause of RA is not fully understood, but a combination of genetic and environmental factors is thought to trigger the immune system's misguided attack on the joints. Once the inflammatory process is set in motion, it can be difficult to control without targeted interventions.

The Systemic Impact of Inflammation in Arthritis

While joint pain and stiffness are the hallmark symptoms of arthritis, the impact of chronic inflammation extends far beyond the joints. Systemic inflammation associated with arthritis can affect multiple organs and systems throughout the body.

For example, people with RA have an increased risk of cardiovascular disease, likely due to the inflammatory burden on the blood vessels. Chronic inflammation can also contribute to fatigue, mood changes, and even cognitive difficulties in some people with arthritis.

This widespread impact of inflammation underscores the importance of managing arthritis not just for joint health, but for overall well-being. Reducing inflammation through targeted therapies and lifestyle changes can help improve symptoms and reduce the risk of complications.

Diet: A Powerful Tool for Managing Inflammation

While medications can be effective in managing arthritis symptoms and slowing disease progression, they often come with side effects and limitations. Fortunately, there is another powerful tool for managing inflammation that is often overlooked: diet.

The foods we eat can have a profound impact on inflammation levels in the body. Some foods, like processed snacks and red meat, can fuel inflammation, while others, like colorful fruits and vegetables, can help calm it.

By making strategic changes to your diet, you can help reduce the inflammatory burden on your joints and throughout your body. An anti-inflammatory diet emphasizes whole, nutrient-dense foods while minimizing processed and inflammatory foods.

In the following chapters, we'll take a deep dive into the power of an anti-inflammatory diet for managing arthritis. You'll learn which foods to embrace and which to avoid, as well as practical strategies for making lasting changes to your eating habits.

While an anti-inflammatory diet is not a cure for arthritis, it can be a powerful complement to conventional treatments and a key component of a holistic approach to managing the condition. By understanding the role of inflammation in arthritis and taking steps to reduce it through your diet, you can take control of your symptoms and start living your best life.

Chapter 2: The Power of an Anti-Inflammatory Diet

2.1 How diet impacts inflammation levels

The Power of Nutrition

When it comes to managing arthritis symptoms and reducing inflammation, the power of nutrition cannot be overstated. The foods we consume on a daily basis can either fuel the fires of inflammation or help extinguish them. By understanding how different types of foods affect our bodies, we can make informed choices that promote joint health and overall well-being.

The Western Diet: A Recipe for Inflammation

In today's fast-paced world, it's all too easy to fall into the trap of consuming a Western-style diet filled with processed foods, refined sugars, and unhealthy fats. These foods, while convenient and often tasty, can wreak havoc on our bodies and contribute to chronic inflammation.

- Processed foods, such as packaged snacks, frozen dinners, and fast food, are often high in inflammatory compounds like trans fats, refined carbohydrates, and artificial additives. These substances can trigger the release of pro-inflammatory chemicals in the body, leading to increased pain and stiffness in the joints.

-

- Sugar, in particular, is a major culprit when it comes to inflammation. When we consume foods high in added sugars, our blood sugar levels spike, causing the body to release inflammatory messengers called cytokines. Over time, this constant barrage of sugar-induced inflammation can worsen arthritis symptoms and accelerate joint damage.

-

- Unhealthy fats, like the saturated fats found in red meat and full-fat dairy products, can also contribute to inflammation. These fats can trigger the production of prostaglandins, hormone-like substances that promote inflammation throughout the body.

The Anti-Inflammatory Diet: A Natural Approach to Reducing Inflammation

On the flip side, an anti-inflammatory diet emphasizes foods that naturally reduce inflammation in the body. This approach to eating focuses on whole, nutrient-dense foods that are rich in vitamins, minerals, and beneficial plant compounds.

One of the key components of an anti-inflammatory diet is an abundance of colorful fruits and vegetables. These plant-based foods are packed with antioxidants and phytochemicals that help neutralize harmful free radicals and reduce inflammation. Leafy greens, berries, and bright orange and yellow vegetables are all excellent choices.

Whole grains, like brown rice, quinoa, and whole wheat, are also an important part of an anti-inflammatory diet. These complex carbohydrates are rich in fiber, which helps regulate blood sugar levels and reduce inflammation. They also provide a steady source of energy without the inflammatory spikes associated with refined carbs.

Healthy fats, like those found in fatty fish, nuts, seeds, and olive oil, are another crucial component of an anti-inflammatory diet. Omega-3 fatty acids, in particular, have been shown to have potent anti-inflammatory effects in the body. These beneficial fats help counteract the production of inflammatory chemicals and may even help reduce joint pain and stiffness.

Herbs and spices, like ginger, turmeric, and garlic, also have powerful anti-inflammatory properties. These flavorful additions to meals can help reduce inflammation throughout the body and may even have pain-relieving effects.

Making the Switch: Practical Tips for Adopting an Anti-Inflammatory Diet

Transitioning to an anti-inflammatory diet may seem daunting at first, but it doesn't have to be an all-or-nothing proposition. Small, gradual changes can add up to big results over time.

Start by incorporating more fruits and vegetables into your meals and snacks. Aim for a rainbow of colors to ensure you're getting a wide range of anti-inflammatory nutrients. Swap out refined grains for whole grain options, and choose lean proteins like fish, poultry, and legumes over red meat.

When it comes to fats, focus on sources of healthy, anti-inflammatory fats like avocados, nuts, seeds, and olive oil. Limit your intake of saturated and trans fats, which can contribute to inflammation.

Don't be afraid to experiment with new herbs and spices in your cooking. These flavorful additions can help you cut back on salt and sugar while providing a tasty dose of anti-inflammatory benefits.

Remember, small changes can make a big difference over time. By gradually shifting your diet towards more anti-inflammatory foods, you can help reduce inflammation, manage your arthritis symptoms, and improve your overall health and well-being. In the following chapters, we'll dive deeper into specific food groups and nutrients that can help you take control of your arthritis through the power of nutrition.

2.2 Benefits of eating anti-inflammatory foods

Reduced Joint Pain and Stiffness

One of the most significant benefits of adopting an anti-inflammatory diet is the potential for reduced joint pain and stiffness. By consuming foods that naturally combat inflammation, you can help alleviate the discomfort and limitations that come with arthritis.

Anti-inflammatory foods, such as fatty fish, leafy greens, and berries, are rich in nutrients that help regulate the body's inflammatory response. Omega-3 fatty acids, found in abundance in fish like salmon and sardines, have been shown to reduce joint tenderness and morning stiffness in people with rheumatoid arthritis.

Antioxidants, like vitamin C and beta-carotene, are also powerful inflammation fighters. These nutrients help neutralize harmful free radicals that can contribute to joint damage and inflammation. Colorful fruits and vegetables, like spinach, kale, and bell peppers, are excellent sources of these beneficial compounds.

By consistently choosing foods that reduce inflammation and limiting those that promote it, you can help manage your arthritis symptoms and improve your overall joint health. Many people who adopt an anti-inflammatory diet report significant reductions in pain and stiffness, allowing them to move more freely and comfortably throughout their day.

Improved Mobility and Function

In addition to reducing joint pain and stiffness, an anti-inflammatory diet can also help improve mobility and function. When your joints are less inflamed, they can move more easily and with less discomfort. This increased mobility can make a world of difference in your ability to perform daily tasks and engage in the activities you enjoy.

For example, if you've been struggling to open jars or grip objects due to arthritis pain in your hands, the reduced inflammation from an anti-inflammatory diet may help improve your dexterity and grip strength. If knee pain has been making it difficult to climb stairs or take walks, the decreased inflammation and increased joint function may help you move with greater ease and confidence.

By nourishing your body with anti-inflammatory foods, you're not only reducing pain, but also supporting the overall health and function of your joints. This improved joint function can help you maintain your independence, engage in your favorite hobbies, and enjoy a better quality of life.

Boosted Energy and Vitality

Chronic inflammation not only affects your joints but can also take a toll on your overall energy levels and sense of well-being. When your body is constantly battling inflammation, it can leave you feeling fatigued, sluggish, and run down.

An anti-inflammatory diet, on the other hand, can help boost your energy and vitality. By reducing the inflammatory burden on your body, you're allowing your systems to function more efficiently and effectively. When you're not expending so much energy fighting inflammation, you may find that you have more stamina and vibrancy throughout the day.

Many anti-inflammatory foods, like whole grains, legumes, and lean proteins, also provide a steady source of energy without the crashes associated with inflammatory foods like refined carbs and added sugars. By fueling your body with nutrient-dense, anti-inflammatory foods, you're giving yourself the sustenance you need to tackle your day with greater ease and enthusiasm.

Reduced Risk of Other Chronic Diseases

While the primary focus of an anti-inflammatory diet for arthritis is to manage joint symptoms, this way of eating also offers significant benefits for overall health and disease prevention. Chronic inflammation has been linked to a wide range of health problems beyond arthritis, including heart disease, diabetes, and certain cancers.

By adopting an anti-inflammatory diet, you're not only taking steps to manage your arthritis but also reducing your risk of developing these other serious health conditions. The same foods that help combat inflammation in your joints also support the health of your heart, brain, and other vital organs.

For example, the omega-3 fatty acids found in fatty fish and the monounsaturated fats in olive oil and nuts have been shown to promote heart health and reduce the risk of cardiovascular disease. The antioxidants in colorful fruits and vegetables help protect against cellular damage that can contribute to cancer development.

By choosing an anti-inflammatory diet, you're investing in your overall health and well-being, not just your joint health. This holistic approach to nutrition can help you feel your best and reduce your risk of chronic diseases that can compromise your quality of life.

Enhanced Sense of Empowerment and Control

Perhaps one of the most significant benefits of adopting an anti-inflammatory diet is the sense of empowerment and control it can provide. When you're living with a chronic condition like arthritis, it's easy to feel like your health is out of your hands. Conventional treatments, while important, can sometimes leave you feeling like a passive recipient of care rather than an active participant in your own well-being.

By embracing an anti-inflammatory diet, you're taking a proactive role in managing your arthritis symptoms and overall health. Every meal and snack becomes an opportunity to nourish your body and support your joints. You're no longer just relying on medication or waiting for your next doctor's appointment to feel better – you're taking charge of your health on a daily basis.

This sense of empowerment can be incredibly motivating and rewarding. As you start to experience the benefits of an anti-inflammatory diet, like reduced pain and increased mobility, you may find yourself feeling more confident and in control of your health. This newfound sense of agency can spill over into other areas of your life, inspiring you to make positive changes and pursue the things that matter most to you.

Adopting an anti-inflammatory diet is not always easy, and there may be challenges and setbacks along the way. But by staying committed to nourishing your body with the foods that support your health, you're giving yourself the tools and the power to live your best life with arthritis. In the following chapters, we'll explore specific anti-inflammatory foods and strategies to help you make this way of eating a sustainable and enjoyable part of your life.

2.3 Success stories of people who used diet to manage arthritis

Sarah's Story: Reclaiming Her Active Lifestyle

Sarah, a 62-year-old retired teacher, had always been an active person. She enjoyed gardening, taking long walks with her friends, and playing with her grandchildren. However, when osteoarthritis began to take its toll, Sarah found herself struggling with daily tasks and unable to engage in the activities she loved.

The pain and stiffness in her knees and hands made even simple movements, like getting dressed or preparing meals, a challenge. Sarah tried various medications and treatments, but the side effects left her feeling frustrated and hopeless.

It wasn't until Sarah discovered the power of an anti-inflammatory diet that she began to see a real change in her symptoms. She started incorporating more fruits, vegetables, whole grains, and healthy fats into her meals, while reducing her intake of processed foods and red meat.

At first, the changes felt overwhelming, but Sarah found that with a little planning and creativity, she could still enjoy delicious, satisfying meals. She experimented with new recipes and discovered a love for colorful salads and hearty soups.

As the weeks passed, Sarah began to notice a difference in her body. Her joint pain and stiffness started to diminish, and she found herself moving with greater ease. She was able to take longer walks and even return to her beloved garden.

Today, Sarah continues to follow an anti-inflammatory diet and has found a renewed sense of vitality and independence. She's able to keep up with her grandkids and enjoy the active lifestyle she thought she had lost to arthritis.

"I never imagined that something as simple as changing my diet could make such a profound difference in my life," Sarah shares. "It's given me a sense of control over my health and the ability to do the things I love again."

John's Journey: Finding Relief and Renewed Purpose

John, a 58-year-old marketing executive, had always been a high-achiever. He thrived on the fast-paced nature of his work and took pride in his ability to tackle any challenge. However, when rheumatoid arthritis entered the picture, John found himself struggling to keep up.

The pain and inflammation in his joints made it difficult to type on his computer or even hold a pen. He found himself exhausted and frustrated, unable to perform at the level he was used to.

John tried various medications, but the side effects left him feeling foggy and disconnected. He knew he needed to find a better way to manage his symptoms if he wanted to continue his career and maintain his quality of life.

That's when John learned about the anti-inflammatory diet. He was skeptical at first, but with the encouragement of his wife, he decided to give it a try. John began incorporating more fatty fish, like salmon and sardines, into his meals, along with plenty of leafy greens and colorful vegetables.

He also started paying closer attention to his snacks, swapping out processed chips and crackers for nuts, seeds, and fresh fruit. John found that with a little creativity, he could still enjoy satisfying meals and snacks while following an anti-inflammatory approach.

As John stuck with the diet, he began to notice improvements in his symptoms. His joint pain and stiffness started to decrease, and he found himself with more energy and focus throughout the day. He was able to return to his work with renewed vigor and even took up cycling as a low-impact form of exercise.

"Adopting an anti-inflammatory diet has been a game-changer for me," John explains. "It's not just about reducing my arthritis symptoms, but about reclaiming my sense of purpose and vitality. I feel like I'm back in control of my health and my life."

Mary's Transformation: Overcoming Limitations and Embracing Joy

Mary, a 71-year-old grandmother and retired nurse, had always been the caretaker in her family. She was the one her loved ones turned to for support and guidance. However, when osteoarthritis began to limit her mobility and independence, Mary found herself struggling with feelings of helplessness and frustration.

The pain in her hips and knees made it difficult to perform even basic self-care tasks, like bathing and dressing. Mary relied on her daughter for assistance and felt guilty for being a burden on her family.

Despite trying various medications and treatments, Mary found little relief. She began to resign herself to a life of limitations and chronic pain.

It was Mary's granddaughter who first introduced her to the concept of an anti-inflammatory diet. Together, they began exploring new recipes and ingredients, focusing on whole, unprocessed foods like fruits, vegetables, whole grains, and lean proteins.

Mary found joy in discovering new flavors and experimenting with different spices and herbs. She began to look forward to meals as an opportunity to nourish her body and connect with her family.

As Mary embraced the anti-inflammatory diet, she began to notice changes in her body. The pain and stiffness in her joints started to ease, and she found herself moving with greater comfort and confidence.

She was able to regain her independence and even started attending water aerobics classes at her local community center. Mary found a renewed sense of purpose and joy in being able to engage in activities she loved and contribute to her family once again.

"Embracing an anti-inflammatory diet has been a journey of self-discovery and empowerment for me," Mary shares. "It's not just about reducing my arthritis symptoms, but about rediscovering my joy and purpose in life. I feel like I've been given a second chance to live life on my own terms."

These success stories demonstrate the profound impact that an anti-inflammatory diet can have on the lives of people with arthritis. By nourishing their bodies with whole, anti-inflammatory foods, Sarah, John, and Mary were able to reduce their symptoms, regain their independence, and reclaim the activities and relationships that bring them joy.

Their stories serve as a reminder that while arthritis can feel like an overwhelming and isolating condition, there is hope for a better quality of life. By embracing the power of nutrition and making sustainable changes to their diets, people with arthritis can take control of their health and find relief from the limitations and pain that have held them back.

In the following chapters, we'll explore the specific foods and strategies that can help you harness the anti-inflammatory power of nutrition and create your own success story in managing arthritis.

Part II: The Anti-Inflammatory Kitchen

Chapter 3: Anti-Inflammatory Foods to Embrace

3.1 Vegetables and fruits

The Powerhouses of Anti-Inflammatory Nutrition

When it comes to adopting an anti-inflammatory diet for managing arthritis, vegetables and fruits are the undisputed stars of the show. These nutrient-dense foods are packed with vitamins, minerals, antioxidants, and fiber that work together to reduce inflammation, support joint health, and promote overall well-being.

The vibrant colors of fruits and vegetables are not just visually appealing; they also signify the presence of powerful anti-inflammatory compounds. From the deep greens of spinach and kale to the bright reds of tomatoes and berries, each color represents a unique set of phytochemicals that offer specific health benefits.

Embracing a Rainbow of Fruits and Veggies

To maximize the anti-inflammatory potential of your diet, aim to incorporate a wide variety of colorful fruits and vegetables into your meals and snacks. By eating a rainbow of produce, you ensure that you're getting a diverse array of nutrients and antioxidants that work synergistically to combat inflammation.

Leafy greens, like spinach, kale, collard greens, and Swiss chard, are particularly potent inflammation fighters. These nutritional powerhouses are rich in vitamins A, C, and K, as well as minerals like calcium and magnesium. They also contain plant compounds called flavonoids that have been shown to reduce inflammation and oxidative stress in the body.

Brightly colored fruits, like berries, oranges, and papaya, are also excellent choices for an anti-inflammatory diet. Berries, in particular, are loaded with anthocyanins, a type of antioxidant that gives them their deep red, purple, and blue hues. These compounds have been found to inhibit the production of inflammatory chemicals in the body, helping to reduce joint pain and stiffness.

Other anti-inflammatory superstars in the fruit and vegetable realm include:

- Cruciferous vegetables, like broccoli, cauliflower, and Brussels sprouts, which contain sulforaphane, a compound that helps reduce inflammation and protects against cellular damage.

- Alliums, like garlic and onions, which contain organosulfur compounds that have anti-inflammatory and immune-boosting properties.
- Tomatoes, which are rich in lycopene, a potent antioxidant that has been shown to reduce inflammation and oxidative stress in the body.
- Avocados, which are packed with heart-healthy monounsaturated fats, fiber, and vitamin E, all of which contribute to their anti-inflammatory effects.

Practical Strategies for Incorporating More Produce

While the benefits of fruits and vegetables are clear, many people struggle to incorporate enough of these nutritional powerhouses into their diets. Here are some practical strategies for boosting your intake of anti-inflammatory produce:

- Make fruits and veggies the star of your plate. Aim to fill at least half of your plate with a variety of colorful fruits and vegetables at each meal.
- Embrace convenience. Keep pre-washed, pre-cut fruits and veggies on hand for easy snacking and meal prep. Frozen fruits and vegetables are also great options, as they are often just as nutritious as their fresh counterparts.
- Get creative with your cooking. Try new recipes that showcase the flavors and textures of different fruits and vegetables. Experiment with roasting, grilling, sautéing, and stir-frying to keep things interesting.
- Sneak them into your favorite dishes. Add grated zucchini or carrots to meatballs or pasta sauces, blend spinach into smoothies, or top pizzas with arugula and roasted red peppers.
- Make them portable. Pack sliced fruits and veggies, like carrot sticks, cucumber rounds, and apple slices, for on-the-go snacks. Pair them with hummus, guacamole, or nut butter for a satisfying and anti-inflammatory treat.

The Anti-Inflammatory Potential of Produce

By making fruits and vegetables the foundation of your anti-inflammatory diet, you're not only providing your body with the nutrients it needs to combat inflammation but also supporting overall health and well-being.

The fiber in fruits and vegetables helps promote healthy digestion, which is essential for reducing inflammation in the gut and throughout the body. Fiber also helps regulate blood sugar levels, which can be important for managing inflammation associated with conditions like diabetes and metabolic syndrome.

The antioxidants in fruits and vegetables, like vitamin C and beta-carotene, help protect cells from oxidative damage that can contribute to inflammation and joint degeneration. These nutrients also support the health of the immune system, which plays a key role in regulating inflammation in the body.

Furthermore, many fruits and vegetables contain compounds that have been shown to directly inhibit the production of inflammatory chemicals in the body. For example, quercetin, a flavonoid found in apples, onions, and berries, has been found to block the production of pro-inflammatory substances like leukotrienes and prostaglandins.

The Takeaway

Incorporating a wide variety of colorful fruits and vegetables into your anti-inflammatory diet is one of the most powerful steps you can take to manage arthritis symptoms and promote overall health. By making these nutritional powerhouses the foundation of your meals and snacks, you're providing your body with the tools it needs to combat inflammation, reduce joint pain and stiffness, and support long-term well-being.

While changing your diet can feel overwhelming at times, remember that every small step counts. Start by adding one extra serving of fruits or vegetables to your diet each day, and gradually work your way up to filling half your plate with these anti-inflammatory superstars at each meal.

With a little creativity and a willingness to experiment, you'll soon discover a world of delicious and nourishing recipes that showcase the incredible potential of fruits and vegetables in managing arthritis and promoting vibrant health.

3.2 Whole grains

The Unsung Heroes of an Anti-Inflammatory Diet

When it comes to adopting an anti-inflammatory diet for managing arthritis, whole grains are often the unsung heroes. While fruits and vegetables tend to get the most attention for their anti-inflammatory properties, whole grains play an equally important role in reducing inflammation and supporting overall health.

Whole grains are exactly what they sound like – grains that have been minimally processed and retain all three parts of the original kernel: the bran, germ, and endosperm. This is in contrast to refined grains, which have had the bran and germ removed, leaving only the starchy endosperm.

The Power of Fiber and Phytochemicals

One of the key reasons whole grains are so beneficial for reducing inflammation is their high fiber content. The bran and germ of whole grains are rich in both insoluble and soluble fiber, which help regulate digestion, promote feelings of fullness, and support the growth of beneficial gut bacteria.

A healthy gut microbiome is essential for reducing inflammation throughout the body. When the balance of gut bacteria is disrupted, it can lead to increased intestinal permeability, or "leaky gut," which allows inflammatory compounds to enter the bloodstream and contribute to systemic inflammation.

In addition to fiber, whole grains are also packed with anti-inflammatory phytochemicals, like polyphenols and lignans. These plant compounds act as antioxidants in the body, helping to neutralize harmful free radicals that can contribute to inflammation and cellular damage.

Some of the most potent anti-inflammatory whole grains include:

- Oats: Rich in beta-glucan, a type of soluble fiber that has been shown to reduce inflammation and improve heart health.
- Brown rice: Contains lignans and magnesium, both of which have anti-inflammatory properties.
- Quinoa: A complete protein that's high in fiber and antioxidants like quercetin and kaempferol.
- Barley: Rich in beta-glucans and lignans, which have been shown to reduce inflammation and support gut health.
- Whole wheat: Contains lignans and vitamin E, both of which have anti-inflammatory effects.

Practical Strategies for Incorporating More Whole Grains

While the benefits of whole grains are clear, many people struggle to incorporate them into their diets regularly. Here are some practical strategies for boosting your intake of anti-inflammatory whole grains:

- Choose whole grain bread, pasta, and cereals over their refined counterparts. Look for products that list a whole grain, like whole wheat or brown rice, as the first ingredient.
- Experiment with ancient grains, like quinoa, millet, and sorghum. These nutrient-dense grains offer a variety of flavors and textures and can be used in place of rice or pasta in many recipes.
- Add whole grains to salads and soups. Toss cooked quinoa or barley into your favorite salad, or add a handful of oats to your next batch of vegetable soup.
- Make your own granola or energy bars using whole grain oats, nuts, and dried fruit. This allows you to control the ingredients and avoid added sugars and inflammatory oils.
- Try whole grain breakfast bowls. Top cooked oats or quinoa with fresh fruit, nuts, and a drizzle of honey for a satisfying and anti-inflammatory breakfast.

The Glycemic Index and Inflammation

Another important consideration when incorporating whole grains into an anti-inflammatory diet is the glycemic index (GI). The GI is a measure of how quickly a food raises blood sugar levels after consumption. Foods with a high GI, like refined carbohydrates, cause rapid spikes in blood sugar, which can trigger inflammation in the body.

Whole grains tend to have a lower GI than refined grains, thanks to their high fiber content. Fiber helps slow the absorption of sugar into the bloodstream, preventing the inflammatory spikes associated with high GI foods.

However, it's important to note that not all whole grains are created equal when it comes to the GI. Some, like brown rice and whole wheat bread, still have a relatively high GI compared to other whole grain options.

To keep inflammation at bay, focus on incorporating low GI whole grains, like oats, barley, and quinoa, into your diet regularly. Pairing whole grains with protein and healthy fats can also help slow the absorption of sugar and reduce the inflammatory impact.

The Takeaway

Whole grains are a crucial component of an anti-inflammatory diet for managing arthritis. By providing the body with fiber, antioxidants, and anti-inflammatory phytochemicals, whole grains help reduce systemic inflammation, support gut health, and promote overall well-being.

To reap the benefits of whole grains, aim to incorporate a variety of minimally processed options into your diet regularly. Choose products that list a whole grain as the first ingredient, experiment with ancient grains, and focus on low GI options like oats and barley.

Remember, swapping refined grains for whole grains doesn't have to be an all-or-nothing proposition. Start by making small changes, like choosing whole grain bread over white or adding a handful of oats to your morning smoothie. Over time, these small shifts can add up to big benefits for your joint health and overall well-being.

By making whole grains a staple of your anti-inflammatory diet, you'll be providing your body with the nutrients it needs to combat inflammation, reduce joint pain and stiffness, and promote long-term health. So, the next time you reach for a grain, choose whole – your joints will thank you.

3.3 Healthy fats

The Surprising Inflammation Fighters

When it comes to managing arthritis through an anti-inflammatory diet, healthy fats are an essential piece of the puzzle. For years, fat was vilified as a dietary villain, but we now know that not all fats are created equal. In fact, certain types of fat can be powerful allies in the fight against inflammation and joint pain.

Healthy fats, also known as unsaturated fats, include both monounsaturated and polyunsaturated fats. These fats are liquid at room temperature and are found in a variety of plant-based foods and fatty fish.

The Anti-Inflammatory Power of Omega-3s

One of the most potent types of healthy fat for reducing inflammation is omega-3 fatty acids. These polyunsaturated fats are found in high concentrations in fatty fish, like salmon, sardines, and mackerel, as well as in plant sources like flaxseeds, chia seeds, and walnuts.

Omega-3s work their anti-inflammatory magic by reducing the production of inflammatory compounds in the body, like cytokines and eicosanoids. They also help regulate the immune system, which can be overactive in people with autoimmune forms of arthritis like rheumatoid arthritis.

Studies have shown that regular consumption of omega-3s can help reduce joint pain, stiffness, and swelling in people with rheumatoid arthritis. Some research even suggests that omega-3s may help reduce the need for anti-inflammatory medications in some people.

To reap the benefits of omega-3s, aim to include fatty fish in your diet at least twice a week. If you're not a fan of fish, consider taking a high-quality omega-3 supplement, like fish oil or algae oil.

The Versatility of Monounsaturated Fats

Another type of healthy fat that can be beneficial for managing arthritis is monounsaturated fat. This type of fat is found in high concentrations in foods like olive oil, avocados, nuts, and seeds.

Monounsaturated fats have been shown to reduce inflammation and improve heart health. They may also help improve joint function and reduce pain in people with osteoarthritis.

One of the best sources of monounsaturated fats is extra virgin olive oil. This flavorful oil is a staple of the Mediterranean diet, which has been associated with reduced inflammation and improved overall health.

To incorporate more monounsaturated fats into your diet, try using olive oil as your primary cooking oil, snacking on a handful of nuts or seeds, or adding sliced avocado to your salads and sandwiches.

The Balancing Act of Omega-6s

While omega-3s are the star of the anti-inflammatory fat world, it's important not to overlook their cousin, omega-6 fatty acids. These polyunsaturated fats are found in high concentrations in vegetable oils, like soybean, corn, and sunflower oil, as well as in many processed foods.

Unlike omega-3s, which are anti-inflammatory, omega-6s can actually promote inflammation in the body when consumed in excess. The problem is that the Western diet tends to be much higher in omega-6s than omega-3s, with some estimates suggesting a ratio of 20:1 or higher.

To keep inflammation at bay, it's important to strive for a more balanced ratio of omega-6s to omega-3s, ideally around 4:1 or lower. This means reducing your intake of processed foods and vegetable oils and increasing your intake of omega-3-rich foods like fatty fish and flaxseeds.

Practical Strategies for Incorporating Healthy Fats

While the benefits of healthy fats are clear, many people struggle to incorporate them into their diets in a balanced way. Here are some practical strategies for boosting your intake of anti-inflammatory fats:

- Use olive oil as your primary cooking oil. Extra virgin olive oil is a great choice for sautéing, roasting, and dressing salads.

- Snack on a handful of nuts or seeds each day. Walnuts, almonds, and pumpkin seeds are all great sources of healthy fats.
- Add fatty fish to your diet at least twice a week. Try salmon, sardines, or mackerel, either fresh or canned.
- Incorporate avocado into your meals. Add sliced avocado to salads, sandwiches, or smoothies for a creamy, satisfying source of monounsaturated fat.
- Sprinkle ground flaxseeds or chia seeds into your oatmeal, yogurt, or smoothies. These tiny seeds are packed with omega-3s and fiber.

The Takeaway

Healthy fats are an essential component of an anti-inflammatory diet for managing arthritis. By incorporating omega-3-rich foods like fatty fish and flaxseeds, monounsaturated fats like olive oil and avocados, and reducing your intake of omega-6-heavy processed foods, you can help reduce inflammation, improve joint function, and promote overall health.

Remember, fat is not the enemy – it's all about choosing the right types of fat and incorporating them into your diet in a balanced way. By making healthy fats a regular part of your anti-inflammatory eating plan, you'll be providing your body with the tools it needs to combat inflammation, reduce joint pain and stiffness, and promote long-term well-being.

So, don't be afraid to embrace the power of healthy fats. Your joints (and your taste buds) will thank you.

3.4 Lean proteins

The Building Blocks of a Healthy, Anti-Inflammatory Diet

Protein is an essential macronutrient that plays a crucial role in building and repairing tissues, supporting immune function, and maintaining muscle mass. When it comes to managing arthritis through an anti-inflammatory diet, choosing the right types of protein can make a significant difference in your overall health and well-being.

Lean proteins, in particular, are an important part of an anti-inflammatory eating plan. These proteins are lower in saturated fat and calories than their high-fat counterparts, making them a heart-healthy choice for people with arthritis, who may be at increased risk for cardiovascular disease.

The Benefits of Fish and Seafood

One of the best sources of lean protein for an anti-inflammatory diet is fish and seafood. Fatty fish, like salmon, mackerel, and sardines, are particularly beneficial, as they are rich in omega-3 fatty acids, which have potent anti-inflammatory properties.

In addition to their omega-3 content, fish and seafood are also excellent sources of vitamins and minerals that support overall health. For example, oysters are one of the best dietary sources of zinc, a mineral that plays a key role in immune function and wound healing.

To reap the benefits of fish and seafood, aim to include them in your diet at least twice a week. Choose a variety of options, including both fatty and lean fish, to ensure you're getting a diverse array of nutrients.

The Power of Plant-Based Proteins

While fish and seafood are excellent sources of lean protein, they're not the only options for an anti-inflammatory diet. Plant-based proteins, like legumes, nuts, and seeds, can also be powerful allies in the fight against inflammation.

Legumes, which include beans, lentils, and peas, are not only rich in protein but also high in fiber and antioxidants. These nutrients work together to promote healthy digestion, regulate blood sugar levels, and reduce inflammation throughout the body.

Nuts and seeds, like almonds, walnuts, and pumpkin seeds, are also excellent sources of plant-based protein. These nutrient-dense foods are rich in healthy fats, fiber, and minerals like magnesium and zinc, which support overall health and well-being.

To incorporate more plant-based proteins into your diet, try adding a handful of nuts or seeds to your morning oatmeal or yogurt, tossing some chickpeas or lentils into your salads, or using hummus or nut butter as a dip for raw veggies.

The Importance of Lean Meats

While plant-based proteins and fish are often emphasized in an anti-inflammatory diet, lean meats can also be a part of a healthy eating plan. Poultry, like chicken and turkey, and lean cuts of beef and pork are all excellent sources of protein that can help support muscle health and immune function.

When choosing meats, it's important to opt for lean cuts and to prepare them in a healthy way. Skinless chicken breast, turkey tenderloin, and sirloin steak are all lean options that can be grilled, baked, or stir-fried with vegetables for a nutritious meal.

It's also important to limit your intake of processed meats, like bacon, sausage, and deli meats, which are often high in saturated fat and sodium and may contribute to inflammation in the body.

Practical Strategies for Incorporating Lean Proteins

Incorporating lean proteins into your anti-inflammatory diet doesn't have to be complicated. Here are some practical strategies for boosting your intake of these nutritious foods:

-
- Make fish and seafood a regular part of your meal rotation. Experiment with different types of fish and preparation methods to keep things interesting.
- Incorporate plant-based proteins into your meals and snacks. Try a vegetarian chili with kidney beans, a quinoa and chickpea salad, or a snack of roasted pumpkin seeds.

- Choose lean cuts of meat and poultry. Opt for skinless chicken breast, turkey tenderloin, and lean cuts of beef and pork.
- Prepare your proteins in a healthy way. Grill, bake, or stir-fry your meats and seafood with herbs and spices for flavor, rather than breading or frying them.
- Limit your intake of processed meats. Save bacon, sausage, and deli meats for occasional treats rather than making them a regular part of your diet.
- The Takeaway
- Lean proteins are an essential component of an anti-inflammatory diet for managing arthritis. By incorporating a variety of fish, seafood, plant-based proteins, and lean meats into your meals and snacks, you can support muscle health, immune function, and overall well-being.

Remember, the key to a healthy diet is balance and variety. Aim to include a range of lean proteins in your meals, along with plenty of colorful fruits and vegetables, whole grains, and healthy fats.

By making lean proteins a regular part of your anti-inflammatory eating plan, you'll be providing your body with the building blocks it needs to combat inflammation, reduce joint pain and stiffness, and promote long-term health. So, don't be afraid to experiment with new recipes and ingredients – your taste buds (and your joints) will thank you.

3.5 Herbs and spices

The Secret Weapons of an Anti-Inflammatory Diet

When it comes to adopting an anti-inflammatory diet for managing arthritis, herbs and spices are often the unsung heroes. These flavorful additions to your meals not only make your food taste great but also pack a powerful punch when it comes to reducing inflammation and supporting overall health.

Herbs and spices have been used for centuries in traditional medicine systems around the world to treat a variety of ailments, including inflammation and pain. Modern science has begun to validate many of these traditional uses, with research showing that certain herbs and spices contain potent anti-inflammatory compounds.

The Anti-Inflammatory All-Stars

One of the most well-known anti-inflammatory herbs is turmeric. This vibrant yellow spice, commonly used in Indian and Middle Eastern cuisine, contains a compound called curcumin that has been shown to have powerful anti-inflammatory effects in the body.

Curcumin works by inhibiting the production of inflammatory chemicals, like prostaglandins and leukotrienes, and by blocking the activity of enzymes that contribute to inflammation. Some studies have even found that curcumin may be as effective as certain anti-inflammatory drugs in reducing pain and swelling in people with arthritis.

Other anti-inflammatory all-stars in the herb and spice world include:

- Ginger: This warming spice contains compounds called gingerols that have been shown to reduce inflammation and relieve pain in people with osteoarthritis and rheumatoid arthritis.
- Garlic: Rich in sulfur compounds that have anti-inflammatory and immune-boosting properties, garlic has been used for centuries to treat a variety of ailments.
- Cinnamon: This sweet spice contains compounds that help regulate blood sugar levels and reduce inflammation throughout the body.
- Cayenne pepper: The active compound in cayenne, capsaicin, has been shown to have pain-relieving and anti-inflammatory effects.
- Rosemary: This fragrant herb is rich in antioxidants and anti-inflammatory compounds that help protect cells from damage and reduce inflammation.

Practical Strategies for Incorporating More Herbs and Spices

While the benefits of herbs and spices are clear, many people struggle to incorporate them into their diets in a meaningful way. Here are some practical strategies for boosting your intake of these flavorful inflammation fighters:

Experiment with different herbs and spices in your cooking. Try adding turmeric to your scrambled eggs, ginger to your stir-fries, or cinnamon to your morning oatmeal.

Make your own spice blends. Combine your favorite herbs and spices to create custom blends that you can use to flavor your meals. For example, try mixing turmeric, ginger, and cinnamon for a warming, anti-inflammatory blend.

Add herbs and spices to your smoothies. Toss a knob of fresh ginger or a pinch of cayenne into your favorite smoothie recipe for an anti-inflammatory boost.

Sip on herbal teas. Many herbs, like ginger, turmeric, and rosemary, can be brewed into delicious and soothing teas that help reduce inflammation and support overall health.

Use herbs and spices as a replacement for salt. Instead of reaching for the salt shaker, try flavoring your meals with herbs and spices like garlic, rosemary, and thyme.

The Synergistic Power of Herbs and Spices

While individual herbs and spices have potent anti-inflammatory effects, the real magic happens when you combine them. Many herbs and spices have synergistic effects, meaning that they work together to enhance each other's benefits.

For example, black pepper contains a compound called piperine that has been shown to enhance the absorption of curcumin from turmeric. By combining these two spices, you can boost the anti-inflammatory power of your meals.

Similarly, the combination of ginger and turmeric has been found to be more effective at reducing inflammation and relieving pain than either spice alone. This dynamic duo is a common pairing in many traditional medicine systems and can be easily incorporated into your favorite recipes.

The Takeaway

Herbs and spices are a delicious and powerful tool for managing inflammation and supporting overall health in people with arthritis. By incorporating a variety of these flavorful ingredients into your meals and snacks, you can help reduce pain, swelling, and stiffness while enjoying the tasty benefits of a diverse and satisfying diet.

Remember, a little goes a long way when it comes to herbs and spices. You don't need to overload your meals with these ingredients to reap their benefits. Start by experimenting with small amounts and gradually increase your intake as your taste buds adapt.

By making herbs and spices a regular part of your anti-inflammatory eating plan, you'll be providing your body with a natural pharmacy of compounds that work together to combat inflammation, reduce joint pain, and promote long-term health. So, don't be afraid to spice things up in the kitchen – your joints (and your taste buds) will thank you.

Chapter 4: Inflammatory Foods to Avoid

4.1 Processed and refined foods

The Inflammation Culprits Lurking in Your Kitchen

When it comes to managing arthritis through an anti-inflammatory diet, it's not just about what you eat – it's also about what you avoid. Processed and refined foods are some of the biggest culprits when it comes to promoting inflammation in the body, and they can be a major obstacle to finding relief from joint pain and stiffness.

Processed foods are those that have been altered from their natural state for convenience and safety reasons. These foods often come in packages or boxes, have a list of ingredients that includes many hard-to-pronounce items, and have a long shelf life.

Refined foods, on the other hand, are those that have been stripped of their natural nutrients and fiber during processing. These foods are often made with white flour, white sugar, or other refined grains and sugars.

The Inflammatory Effects of Processing and Refining

So why are processed and refined foods so harmful when it comes to inflammation? There are a few key reasons.

First, these foods are often high in unhealthy fats, like trans fats and saturated fats. These fats can trigger the production of inflammatory chemicals in the body, leading to increased pain and swelling in the joints.

Second, processed and refined foods are often high in added sugars. When we consume large amounts of sugar, it can cause our blood sugar levels to spike and then crash, leading to a cascade of inflammatory responses in the body. Over time, this chronic inflammation can worsen arthritis symptoms and even contribute to the development of other chronic diseases.

Third, these foods are often low in essential nutrients, like vitamins, minerals, and fiber. When we don't get enough of these nutrients, our bodies can't function at their best, and we may be more susceptible to inflammation and other health problems.

Common Processed and Refined Foods to Avoid

So what are some of the most common processed and refined foods that people with arthritis should avoid? Here are a few examples:

- Packaged snacks, like chips, crackers, and cookies
- Sugary beverages, like soda and sweetened tea

- White bread, pasta, and other refined grains
- Processed meats, like bacon, sausage, and deli meats
- Frozen dinners and other pre-packaged meals
- Fast food and takeout meals
- Commercially baked goods, like cakes, muffins, and pastries

These foods are often high in unhealthy fats, added sugars, and salt, and low in essential nutrients that our bodies need to function at their best.

The Whole Foods Alternative

So if processed and refined foods are off the table, what should people with arthritis eat instead? The answer is simple: whole, unprocessed foods.

Whole foods are those that are as close to their natural state as possible. They include fresh fruits and vegetables, whole grains, lean proteins, and healthy fats. These foods are packed with the nutrients our bodies need to fight inflammation and promote overall health.

Some examples of whole foods that are particularly beneficial for people with arthritis include:

- Colorful fruits and vegetables, like berries, leafy greens, and sweet potatoes
- Whole grains, like quinoa, brown rice, and rolled oats
- Fatty fish, like salmon, mackerel, and sardines
- Nuts and seeds, like almonds, walnuts, and flaxseeds
- Legumes, like lentils, chickpeas, and black beans
- Healthy oils, like olive oil and avocado oil
- By filling your plate with these whole, unprocessed foods, you'll be providing your body with the tools it needs to fight inflammation and promote overall health.

Practical Strategies for Cutting Back on Processed and Refined Foods

If you're used to eating a lot of processed and refined foods, cutting back can feel overwhelming at first. Here are some practical strategies for making the transition:

- Read labels carefully. When shopping for packaged foods, take a close look at the ingredient list. If you see a lot of hard-to-pronounce items or added sugars, put it back on the shelf.
- Plan your meals ahead of time. By planning out your meals and snacks for the week, you'll be less likely to reach for processed convenience foods when hunger strikes.
- Cook more meals at home. When you cook at home, you have control over the ingredients you use and the cooking methods you employ. Try to cook more meals from scratch using whole, unprocessed ingredients.

- Find healthy substitutes for your favorite treats. If you have a sweet tooth, try satisfying it with fresh fruit or a small piece of dark chocolate instead of sugary snacks or desserts.
- Be mindful of portion sizes. When you do eat processed or refined foods, be mindful of your portion sizes. A small serving of chips or cookies every once in a while is okay – just don't make it a daily habit.

The Takeaway

Processed and refined foods are major contributors to inflammation in the body, and they can be a big obstacle to finding relief from arthritis symptoms. By cutting back on these foods and replacing them with whole, unprocessed alternatives, you can help reduce inflammation, improve joint health, and promote overall well-being.

Remember, making dietary changes can be challenging, especially if you're used to relying on convenience foods. Be patient with yourself and focus on progress, not perfection. Every small step you take towards a more whole foods-based diet is a step in the right direction for your health and your arthritis management plan.

So next time you're at the grocery store or planning your meals for the week, keep these tips in mind. Your joints (and your taste buds) will thank you for making the switch to a more anti-inflammatory way of eating.

4.2 Unhealthy fats

The Hidden Dangers in Your Favorite Foods

When it comes to managing arthritis through diet, not all fats are created equal. While some types of fat, like omega-3 fatty acids, can actually help reduce inflammation in the body, other types of fat can have the opposite effect, triggering inflammation and worsening joint pain and stiffness.

Unhealthy fats, also known as "bad" fats, include saturated fats and trans fats. These fats are commonly found in processed and fried foods, as well as in certain types of meat and dairy products.

The Inflammatory Effects of Saturated Fats

Saturated fats are those that are solid at room temperature, like butter, lard, and coconut oil. These fats are also found in high amounts in fatty cuts of meat, full-fat dairy products, and many processed foods.

When consumed in excess, saturated fats can contribute to inflammation in the body. They do this by triggering the production of inflammatory chemicals called cytokines, which can worsen joint pain and stiffness in people with arthritis.

In addition to their inflammatory effects, saturated fats can also contribute to other health problems, like heart disease and high cholesterol. For people with arthritis, who may already be at increased risk for these conditions, limiting saturated fat intake is especially important.

The Dangers of Trans Fats

Trans fats are a type of unsaturated fat that have been chemically altered to increase their shelf life and stability. These fats are commonly found in processed foods like crackers, cookies, and fried foods, as well as in some margarines and vegetable shortenings.

Like saturated fats, trans fats can trigger inflammation in the body, worsening joint pain and stiffness in people with arthritis. But the dangers of trans fats go beyond their inflammatory effects.

Trans fats have been shown to increase the risk of heart disease, stroke, and type 2 diabetes, even in small amounts. In fact, the evidence against trans fats is so strong that the FDA has banned their use in most foods, starting in 2018.

Common Sources of Unhealthy Fats

So where are these unhealthy fats hiding in your diet? Here are some common sources to watch out for:

- Fatty cuts of meat, like ribeye steak, lamb chops, and pork belly
- Full-fat dairy products, like whole milk, cheese, and ice cream
- Fried foods, like french fries, fried chicken, and doughnuts
- Processed snacks, like crackers, cookies, and pastries
- Vegetable shortenings and some margarines
- Coconut and palm oil

While it may be difficult to eliminate these foods from your diet entirely, cutting back on your intake and replacing them with healthier options can go a long way in reducing inflammation and improving your arthritis symptoms.

The Healthier Fat Alternative

So if unhealthy fats are off the table, what should you be eating instead? The answer is simple: healthy, unsaturated fats.

Unsaturated fats are those that are liquid at room temperature and are found in foods like nuts, seeds, avocados, and fatty fish. These fats have been shown to have anti-inflammatory effects in the body, helping to reduce joint pain and stiffness in people with arthritis.

Some of the best sources of healthy, unsaturated fats include:

- Olive oil
- Avocados
- Nuts and seeds, like almonds, walnuts, and flaxseeds
- Fatty fish, like salmon, mackerel, and sardines

By incorporating these healthy fats into your diet and limiting your intake of unhealthy fats, you can help reduce inflammation in your body and improve your overall health.

Practical Strategies for Cutting Back on Unhealthy Fats

If you're used to eating a lot of foods high in unhealthy fats, cutting back can be a challenge. Here are some practical strategies for making the transition:

- Choose leaner cuts of meat. When buying meat, opt for leaner cuts like chicken breast, turkey, and lean beef, and trim any visible fat before cooking.
- Switch to low-fat or non-fat dairy products. Instead of whole milk and full-fat cheese, choose skim milk, low-fat yogurt, and reduced-fat cheese.
- Use healthier cooking methods. Instead of frying your foods, try baking, grilling, or roasting them instead. When sautéing, use a small amount of olive oil instead of butter or vegetable oil.
- Read labels carefully. When buying packaged foods, check the label for saturated and trans fat content. Choose products with the lowest amounts of these unhealthy fats.
- Embrace healthy fat sources. Incorporate more nuts, seeds, avocados, and fatty fish into your diet to get the anti-inflammatory benefits of healthy, unsaturated fats.

The Takeaway

Unhealthy fats, like saturated and trans fats, can be major contributors to inflammation in the body, worsening joint pain and stiffness in people with arthritis. By cutting back on these fats and replacing them with healthier, unsaturated fats, you can help reduce inflammation and improve your overall health. Remember, making dietary changes can be challenging, especially if you're used to eating a lot of foods high in unhealthy fats. Be patient with yourself and focus on progress, not perfection. Every small step you take towards a healthier diet is a step in the right direction for your arthritis management plan.

So next time you're at the grocery store or cooking a meal, keep these tips in mind. Your joints (and your heart) will thank you for making the switch to a more anti-inflammatory way of eating.

4.3 Added sugars

The Sweet Sabotage of Your Arthritis Diet

When it comes to managing arthritis through diet, many people focus on what they should be eating – plenty of colorful fruits and vegetables, whole grains, lean proteins, and healthy fats. But what about the foods you should be avoiding? One of the biggest culprits when it comes to inflammatory foods is added sugars.

Added sugars are sugars that are added to foods during processing or preparation, as opposed to the natural sugars found in fruits and dairy products. These sugars go by many names, including high fructose corn syrup, cane sugar, honey, and molasses, among others.

The Inflammatory Impact of Added Sugars

So why are added sugars so harmful when it comes to inflammation and arthritis? There are a few key reasons.

First, when we consume foods high in added sugars, our blood sugar levels spike rapidly. This triggers the release of insulin, a hormone that helps shuttle the sugar out of our bloodstream and into our cells. Over time, if we consistently consume a lot of added sugars, our cells can become resistant to insulin, leading to chronic inflammation throughout the body.

This chronic inflammation can worsen joint pain and stiffness in people with arthritis, making it harder to move and perform daily activities. It can also contribute to the development of other chronic diseases, like heart disease and diabetes.

Second, added sugars can contribute to weight gain and obesity, which can put extra stress on already painful joints. Excess weight can also increase inflammation in the body, creating a vicious cycle of pain and immobility.

Finally, many foods high in added sugars are also low in essential nutrients like fiber, vitamins, and minerals. When we fill up on these empty calories, we leave less room for the nutrient-dense foods that can help reduce inflammation and support overall health.

Common Sources of Added Sugars

So where are these added sugars hiding in your diet? Unfortunately, they're pretty much everywhere. Here are some common sources to watch out for:

- Sweetened beverages, like soda, sweet tea, and sports drinks
- Baked goods, like cookies, cakes, and pastries
- Candy and chocolate
- Flavored yogurts and milk products
- Condiments, like ketchup, barbecue sauce, and salad dressings
- Breakfast cereals and granola bars
- Canned fruits and vegetables with added syrups or sauces

While it may be unrealistic (and frankly, no fun) to eliminate all sources of added sugars from your diet, reducing your intake can go a long way in managing inflammation and supporting your overall health.

The Naturally Sweet Solution

So if added sugars are off the table, what can you eat to satisfy your sweet tooth? The answer is simple: whole, natural sources of sweetness, like fruits and vegetables.

Fruits are nature's candy, packed with fiber, vitamins, and antioxidants that can help reduce inflammation and support overall health. While they do contain natural sugars, these sugars are balanced by fiber and other nutrients that help regulate blood sugar levels and prevent the inflammatory spikes associated with added sugars.

Some of the best naturally sweet foods to incorporate into your arthritis-friendly diet include:

- Berries, like strawberries, blueberries, and raspberries
- Citrus fruits, like oranges and grapefruits
- Melons, like watermelon and cantaloupe
- Apples and pears
- Sweet potatoes
- Carrots
- Beets

By focusing on these whole, natural sources of sweetness, you can satisfy your cravings while still supporting your body's anti-inflammatory efforts.

Practical Strategies for Reducing Added Sugars

If you're used to consuming a lot of added sugars, cutting back can be a challenge. Here are some practical strategies for reducing your intake and supporting your arthritis management plan:

- Read labels carefully. When buying packaged foods, check the label for added sugars. Aim for products with the lowest amounts of added sugars, or better yet, none at all.
- Swap out sweetened drinks. Instead of soda or sweet tea, opt for water, unsweetened tea, or sparkling water with a splash of fruit juice.
- Satisfy your sweet tooth with fruit. When you're craving something sweet, reach for a piece of fresh fruit or a handful of frozen berries instead of candy or baked goods.
- Make your own treats. When you make your own baked goods or snacks, you have control over the amount and type of sweetener used. Experiment with natural sweeteners like dates, honey, or maple syrup in moderation.
- Be mindful of portion sizes. When you do indulge in a sweet treat, be mindful of your portion sizes. A small serving of your favorite dessert every once in a while is okay – just don't make it a daily habit.

The Takeaway

Added sugars can be a major contributor to inflammation in the body, worsening joint pain and stiffness in people with arthritis. By reducing your intake of these inflammatory sugars and focusing on whole, natural sources of sweetness, you can support your body's anti-inflammatory efforts and promote overall health.

So next time you're tempted by a sugary treat, remember the impact it can have on your joints and your overall health. By making small, sustainable changes to your diet and focusing on whole, natural foods, you can take control of your arthritis symptoms and live your best, most vibrant life.

4.4 Common trigger foods

The Surprising Culprits Behind Your Arthritis Flare-Ups

When it comes to managing arthritis through diet, it's not just about avoiding the usual suspects like processed foods, unhealthy fats, and added sugars. There are also certain foods that, while seemingly innocuous, can actually trigger inflammation and worsen joint pain in some people with arthritis. These foods are known as "trigger foods."

Trigger foods are different for everyone, and what causes a flare-up in one person may have no effect on another. However, there are some common trigger foods that many people with arthritis report as being problematic.

Nightshade Vegetables: A Controversial Culprit

One group of foods that has been the subject of much debate in the arthritis community is nightshade vegetables. This group includes tomatoes, potatoes, eggplant, and peppers.

Some people with arthritis report that consuming these foods can trigger joint pain and inflammation, while others have no issues with them at all. The theory is that nightshades contain compounds called alkaloids that can contribute to inflammation in some people.

If you suspect that nightshades may be a trigger for you, try eliminating them from your diet for a few weeks and see if you notice a difference in your symptoms. Keep in mind that nightshades are also found in many processed foods, like salsa, ketchup, and marinara sauce, so be sure to read labels carefully.

Gluten: A Common Trigger for Rheumatoid Arthritis

Another common trigger food for people with arthritis, particularly rheumatoid arthritis, is gluten. Gluten is a protein found in wheat, barley, and rye, and it's a common ingredient in many processed foods.

Some studies have suggested that gluten can contribute to inflammation in the body and may worsen symptoms in people with autoimmune conditions like rheumatoid arthritis. In fact, some people with RA have reported significant improvements in their symptoms after adopting a gluten-free diet.

If you suspect that gluten may be a trigger for you, try eliminating it from your diet for a few weeks and see if you notice a difference in your symptoms. Keep in mind that gluten is found in many common foods, like bread, pasta, and baked goods, so it can take some effort to avoid it completely.

Dairy: A Potential Problem for Some

Dairy products, like milk, cheese, and yogurt, are another common trigger food for some people with arthritis. The theory is that dairy contains compounds called casein and whey that can contribute to inflammation in the body.

Some people with arthritis report that eliminating dairy from their diet can help reduce joint pain and stiffness, while others have no issues with it at all. If you suspect that dairy may be a trigger for you, try eliminating it from your diet for a few weeks and see if you notice a difference in your symptoms.

Keep in mind that dairy is also a common ingredient in many processed foods, like baked goods and sauces, so be sure to read labels carefully.

Alcohol: A Double-Edged Sword

While moderate alcohol consumption has been associated with some health benefits, like reduced risk of heart disease, it can also be a trigger for some people with arthritis.

Alcohol can contribute to inflammation in the body and may worsen joint pain and stiffness in some people. It can also interfere with the effectiveness of certain arthritis medications and may increase the risk of side effects.

If you enjoy the occasional drink, it's generally okay to consume alcohol in moderation. However, if you find that even small amounts of alcohol trigger your arthritis symptoms, it may be best to avoid it altogether.

The Importance of Personalization

It's important to remember that trigger foods are highly individual, and what causes a flare-up in one person may have no effect on another. The key is to pay attention to your own body and how it responds to different foods.

One helpful strategy is to keep a food diary, where you record everything you eat and drink, along with any symptoms you experience. Over time, you may start to notice patterns emerge, like increased joint pain after consuming certain foods or beverages.

If you suspect that a particular food may be a trigger for you, try eliminating it from your diet for a few weeks and see if you notice a difference in your symptoms. If you do notice an improvement, you can try reintroducing the food slowly and see how your body responds.

It's also important to remember that eliminating trigger foods is just one piece of the puzzle when it comes to managing arthritis through diet. It's still important to focus on consuming a variety of anti-inflammatory foods, like fruits, vegetables, whole grains, and healthy fats, while limiting your intake of processed foods, unhealthy fats, and added sugars.

The Takeaway

While there are some common trigger foods that many people with arthritis report as being problematic, it's important to remember that everyone is different. What causes a flare-up in one person may have no effect on another.

By paying attention to your own body and how it responds to different foods, you can start to identify your own personal trigger foods and make informed choices about what to include (and exclude) from your diet.

So, the next time you sit down to a meal, take a moment to tune in to your body and how it feels. By making mindful choices about what you put on your plate, you can support your joints, reduce inflammation, and feel your best, one bite at a time.

Chapter 5: Stocking Your Anti-Inflammatory Pantry

5.1 Essentials to always have on hand

Your Anti-Inflammatory Pantry Staples

When it comes to adopting an anti-inflammatory diet for managing arthritis, having a well-stocked pantry is key. By keeping certain essential items on hand at all times, you'll be better equipped to whip up nourishing meals and snacks that support your joint health and overall well-being.

But what exactly should you keep in your anti-inflammatory pantry? Let's take a closer look at some of the essential items to always have on hand.

Fruits and Vegetables: The Foundation of Your Anti-Inflammatory Diet

As we discussed in Chapter 3, fruits and vegetables are the cornerstone of an anti-inflammatory diet. These colorful, nutrient-dense foods are packed with antioxidants, vitamins, and minerals that help combat inflammation and support overall health.

When stocking your pantry, aim to have a variety of shelf-stable and frozen fruits and vegetables on hand. Some great options include:

- Canned tomatoes: These versatile pantry staples can be used in everything from soups and stews to sauces and casseroles. Look for low-sodium varieties when possible.
- Frozen berries: Berries are one of the most antioxidant-rich foods you can eat, and having a stash of frozen berries in your freezer means you can enjoy them year-round. Toss them into smoothies, oatmeal, or yogurt for a quick and easy anti-inflammatory boost.
- Frozen leafy greens: Like berries, leafy greens are packed with anti-inflammatory nutrients, but they can be difficult to keep fresh for long periods of time. Frozen leafy greens, like spinach and kale, are a convenient way to always have these nutritional powerhouses on hand.
- Canned beans: Beans are an excellent source of plant-based protein, fiber, and anti-inflammatory nutrients. Keep a variety of canned beans, like black beans, chickpeas, and kidney beans, in your pantry for quick and easy meals.

Whole Grains: Filling and Anti-Inflammatory

As we learned in Chapter 3, whole grains are an important part of an anti-inflammatory diet. These fiber-rich foods help regulate blood sugar levels, promote healthy digestion, and reduce inflammation throughout the body.

When stocking your pantry, aim to have a variety of whole grains on hand, such as:

- Rolled oats: These versatile whole grains can be used in everything from breakfast porridge to granola bars and baked goods. Look for old-fashioned or steel-cut oats for the most anti-inflammatory benefits.

- Quinoa: This protein-rich seed is technically a pseudocereal, but it's often used in place of grains like rice or pasta. Its nutty flavor and fluffy texture make it a delicious and nutritious addition to any anti-inflammatory meal.

- Brown rice: This whole grain staple is a great base for stir-fries, grain bowls, and side dishes. Keep a big bag of brown rice in your pantry for quick and easy meals.

- Whole grain pasta: When you're craving a comforting bowl of pasta, reach for whole grain varieties like whole wheat or brown rice pasta. These options are higher in fiber and nutrients than their refined counterparts.

Healthy Fats: Flavorful and Anti-Inflammatory

As we discussed in Chapter 3, healthy fats are an important part of an anti-inflammatory diet. These fats, like those found in nuts, seeds, and fatty fish, help reduce inflammation and support overall health.

When stocking your pantry, aim to have a variety of healthy fats on hand, such as:

- Extra virgin olive oil: This flavorful and versatile oil is rich in anti-inflammatory compounds and is a great choice for cooking and dressing salads.

- Avocado oil: Like olive oil, avocado oil is rich in healthy monounsaturated fats and has a high smoke point, making it a great choice for high-heat cooking.

- Nuts and seeds: Keep a variety of nuts and seeds, like almonds, walnuts, chia seeds, and flaxseeds, in your pantry for quick and easy snacks and toppings.

- Canned fatty fish: Fatty fish, like salmon and sardines, are rich in anti-inflammatory omega-3 fatty acids. Keep a few cans of these fish in your pantry for quick and easy meals.

- Herbs and Spices: Flavor Boosters and Inflammation Fighters

As we learned in Chapter 3, herbs and spices are not only flavor boosters but also powerful inflammation fighters. These aromatic ingredients are packed with antioxidants and anti-inflammatory compounds that can help reduce joint pain and stiffness.

When stocking your pantry, aim to have a variety of herbs and spices on hand, such as:

- Turmeric: This bright yellow spice is one of the most potent anti-inflammatory herbs around. Use it to add color and flavor to curries, stews, and rice dishes.

- Ginger: This warming spice has been shown to reduce inflammation and relieve pain in people with osteoarthritis and rheumatoid arthritis. Use it to flavor stir-fries, soups, and teas.

- Garlic: This pungent herb is rich in anti-inflammatory compounds and adds depth and flavor to a wide variety of dishes.

- Cinnamon: This sweet and warming spice has been shown to help regulate blood sugar levels and reduce inflammation throughout the body. Use it to flavor oatmeal, baked goods, and smoothies.

The Takeaway

Stocking your pantry with anti-inflammatory essentials is key to successfully adopting an arthritis-friendly diet. By keeping a variety of fruits, vegetables, whole grains, healthy fats, and herbs and spices on hand, you'll be better equipped to create nourishing meals and snacks that support your joint health and overall well-being.

Remember, everyone's pantry will look a little different depending on their personal preferences and dietary needs. Use this list as a starting point and feel free to customize it to suit your own tastes and lifestyle.

5.2 Ingredient substitutions for inflammatory foods

Making the Swap for Better Joint Health

When it comes to adopting an anti-inflammatory diet for managing arthritis, it's not just about what you add to your plate – it's also about what you take away. As we learned in Chapter 4, certain foods, like processed and refined foods, unhealthy fats, added sugars, and common trigger foods, can contribute to inflammation in the body and worsen joint pain and stiffness.

But let's face it – giving up your favorite foods can be tough, especially if you've been eating them for years. The good news is that with a little creativity and some smart substitutions, you can still enjoy many of your favorite dishes without compromising your joint health.

Swapping Out Refined Grains

As we discussed in Chapter 3, whole grains are an important part of an anti-inflammatory diet. But many of the most common grain-based foods, like bread, pasta, and cereals, are made with refined grains that have been stripped of their fiber and nutrients.

To make the swap, look for whole grain alternatives to your favorite refined grain foods. For example:

- Instead of white bread, choose whole wheat or sprouted grain bread.
- Instead of regular pasta, opt for whole wheat, brown rice, or quinoa pasta.
- Instead of sugary breakfast cereals, try rolled oats or a whole grain granola.

By making these simple swaps, you'll be getting more fiber, vitamins, and minerals in your diet, which can help reduce inflammation and support overall health.

Replacing Unhealthy Fats

As we learned in Chapter 4, unhealthy fats, like saturated and trans fats, can contribute to inflammation in the body. But many of the foods we love, like fried foods, baked goods, and processed snacks, are loaded with these inflammatory fats.

To make the swap, look for healthier alternatives to your favorite high-fat foods. For example:

- Instead of deep-frying your foods, try baking, grilling, or sautéing them with a small amount of olive oil.
- Instead of using butter or margarine in your baking, try substituting with mashed avocado, applesauce, or nut butter.
- Instead of reaching for processed snacks like chips or crackers, try a handful of nuts or seeds, or a piece of fresh fruit.

By replacing unhealthy fats with healthier options, you'll be reducing your intake of inflammatory compounds and supporting your body's natural anti-inflammatory processes.

Cutting Back on Added Sugars

As we discussed in Chapter 4, added sugars can be a major contributor to inflammation in the body. But many of the foods and drinks we enjoy, like soda, baked goods, and flavored yogurts, are loaded with these sweet additives.

To make the swap, look for naturally sweet alternatives to your favorite sugary foods. For example:

- Instead of soda or sweet tea, try sparkling water with a splash of fruit juice or a slice of lemon.
- Instead of sugary baked goods, try making your own treats with natural sweeteners like honey, maple syrup, or dates.
- Instead of flavored yogurts, try plain yogurt with fresh berries or a drizzle of honey.

By cutting back on added sugars and opting for naturally sweet foods instead, you'll be reducing your intake of inflammatory compounds and supporting your body's natural healing processes.

Finding Alternatives to Trigger Foods

As we learned in Chapter 4, certain foods, like dairy, gluten, and nightshade vegetables, can be common triggers for some people with arthritis. If you suspect that a particular food may be contributing to your symptoms, it may be worth experimenting with some alternatives.

For example:

- Instead of cow's milk, try almond, coconut, or oat milk.
- Instead of wheat-based products, try gluten-free alternatives like rice, quinoa, or amaranth.

- Instead of tomatoes and peppers, try other colorful vegetables like carrots, beets, and squash.

Keep in mind that everyone's triggers are different, and what works for one person may not work for another. The key is to pay attention to your body and how it responds to different foods, and to work with a healthcare professional or registered dietitian to develop a personalized plan that works for you.

The Importance of Experimentation

Making the switch to an anti-inflammatory diet can be a process of trial and error, and it may take some time to find the substitutions that work best for you. The key is to approach it with a spirit of experimentation and an open mind.

Don't be afraid to try new foods and recipes, even if they seem a little unfamiliar at first. You may be surprised at how delicious and satisfying some of these anti-inflammatory alternatives can be.

The Takeaway

Adopting an anti-inflammatory diet for managing arthritis doesn't have to mean giving up all of your favorite foods. By making some smart substitutions and experimenting with new ingredients, you can still enjoy many of the dishes you love while supporting your body's natural healing processes.

5.3 Reading labels and choosing products wisely

Becoming a Savvy Anti-Inflammatory Shopper

When it comes to adopting an anti-inflammatory diet for managing arthritis, what you put in your shopping cart matters. But with so many products lining the shelves of the grocery store, it can be tough to know which ones are truly anti-inflammatory and which ones are just masquerading as healthy options.

That's where label reading comes in. By learning how to decipher the information on food packaging, you can make more informed choices about the products you buy and the foods you eat.

The Importance of Ingredient Lists

One of the most important things to look at when choosing products for your anti-inflammatory diet is the ingredient list. This is where you'll find a comprehensive rundown of everything that's inside the package, listed in order of quantity from most to least.

When scanning the ingredient list, look for whole, minimally processed foods like fruits, vegetables, whole grains, lean proteins, and healthy fats. These are the foods that will form the foundation of your anti-inflammatory diet and provide your body with the nutrients it needs to fight inflammation and support overall health.

On the other hand, be wary of products that contain a lot of inflammatory ingredients like refined grains, added sugars, unhealthy fats, and artificial additives. These are the foods that can contribute to inflammation in the body and worsen joint pain and stiffness.

Some specific ingredients to watch out for include:

- Partially hydrogenated oils (trans fats)
- High fructose corn syrup and other added sugars
- Refined grains like white flour and white rice
- Artificial colors, flavors, and preservatives
- MSG and other flavor enhancers

If you see these ingredients listed on a product label, it's best to put it back on the shelf and look for a more anti-inflammatory alternative.

Decoding the Nutrition Facts Panel

In addition to the ingredient list, the Nutrition Facts panel on food packaging can also provide valuable information about a product's anti-inflammatory potential.

One of the first things to look at on the Nutrition Facts panel is the serving size. This will tell you how much of the product constitutes a single serving, which can be helpful for portion control and tracking your intake of certain nutrients.

Next, take a look at the calorie content per serving. While calories aren't the only factor to consider when choosing anti-inflammatory foods, being mindful of your overall calorie intake can be important for maintaining a healthy weight, which is crucial for managing arthritis symptoms.

The Nutrition Facts panel will also list the amount of various nutrients per serving, including fat, cholesterol, sodium, carbohydrates, fiber, sugar, protein, and certain vitamins and minerals.

When choosing products for your anti-inflammatory diet, look for those that are:

- Low in saturated and trans fats
- Low in added sugars
- High in fiber
- Rich in vitamins and minerals like vitamin C, vitamin D, and omega-3 fatty acids

Keep in mind that not all fats are created equal when it comes to inflammation. While saturated and trans fats can contribute to inflammation in the body, healthy fats like those found in nuts, seeds, avocados, and fatty fish can actually help reduce inflammation and support joint health.

Choosing Minimally Processed Foods

In general, the less processed a food is, the more anti-inflammatory it's likely to be. That's because processing can strip away many of the nutrients that make whole foods so beneficial for fighting inflammation, while adding in inflammatory ingredients like refined grains, added sugars, and unhealthy fats.

When shopping for your anti-inflammatory diet, aim to choose minimally processed foods as much as possible. This means opting for whole fruits and vegetables instead of processed snacks, whole grains instead of refined carbs, and fresh or frozen meats and seafood instead of processed deli meats and sausages.

Of course, in our busy modern lives, it's not always possible to avoid processed foods altogether. When you do need to choose packaged products, look for those with short, simple ingredient lists that you can recognize and pronounce. Avoid products with a lot of artificial additives, preservatives, and flavor enhancers, as these can contribute to inflammation in the body.

The Power of Experimentation

While label reading can be a powerful tool for making more informed choices about the foods you eat, it's important to remember that everyone's body is different. What works for one person with arthritis may not work for another, and it may take some trial and error to find the products and foods that make you feel your best.

Don't be afraid to experiment with different brands, flavors, and varieties of anti-inflammatory foods. You may be surprised at how delicious and satisfying some of these options can be, and how much better you feel when you're fueling your body with the nutrients it needs to fight inflammation and support overall health.

The Takeaway

Choosing products wisely is a key component of adopting an anti-inflammatory diet for managing arthritis. By learning how to read labels and decipher ingredient lists and Nutrition Facts panels, you can make more informed choices about the foods you buy and eat.

Remember, the goal is to choose whole, minimally processed foods as much as possible, while limiting your intake of inflammatory ingredients like refined grains, added sugars, unhealthy fats, and artificial additives.

By becoming a savvy anti-inflammatory shopper and experimenting with different products and foods, you'll be well on your way to finding the eating plan that works best for you and your unique needs.

So go ahead and start reading those labels – your joints (and your taste buds) will thank you for making the extra effort to choose products that support your health and well-being. With a little practice and persistence, you'll be a label-reading pro in no time.

Part III: Making the Transition

Chapter 6: Beginner's Guide to Adopting an Anti-Inflammatory Diet

---

6.1 Gradual changes to make for lasting success

The Power of Small, Sustainable Steps

When it comes to adopting an anti-inflammatory diet for managing arthritis, it's easy to feel overwhelmed by all the changes you need to make. After all, overhauling your entire way of eating is no small feat, especially if you've been following the same dietary patterns for years or even decades.

But here's the good news: you don't have to change everything all at once. In fact, trying to do too much too soon is often a recipe for burnout and frustration, leading many people to give up on their anti-inflammatory journey before they even have a chance to see results.

The key to lasting success lies in making small, gradual changes over time. By focusing on one or two manageable goals at a time, you can slowly but surely transform your diet and lifestyle in a way that feels sustainable and achievable.

The Benefits of a Gradual Approach

So why is a gradual approach so effective when it comes to adopting an anti-inflammatory diet? There are a few key reasons.

First, small changes are easier to integrate into your existing routine. If you're used to eating a certain way, trying to overhaul your entire diet overnight can be a major shock to your system (and your taste buds). By making incremental changes, you give yourself time to adjust and adapt, making the transition feel more natural and less disruptive.

Second, gradual changes are more likely to stick in the long run. When you try to change too much at once, it's easy to become overwhelmed and fall back into old habits. But when you focus on one small goal at a time, you build momentum and confidence with each success, making it easier to maintain your progress over the long haul.

Finally, a gradual approach allows you to tailor your anti-inflammatory diet to your unique needs and preferences. Everyone's body is different, and what works for one person may not work for another. By making small changes and paying attention to how your body responds, you can fine-tune your diet in a way that feels good and supports your individual health goals.

Small Changes, Big Impact

So what kinds of small changes can you make to start transitioning to an anti-inflammatory diet? Here are a few ideas to get you started:

- Add one new anti-inflammatory food to your diet each week. Instead of trying to overhaul your entire meal plan at once, focus on incorporating one new food at a time. Maybe you start by adding a handful of berries to your morning oatmeal, or swapping out your usual sandwich bread for a whole grain variety. Over time, these small additions can add up to big changes in your overall diet.

- Swap out one inflammatory food for a healthier alternative. Just as you can add in new anti-inflammatory foods gradually, you can also phase out inflammatory foods one at a time. Maybe you start by replacing your usual afternoon soda with a glass of green tea, or swapping out your nightly bowl of ice cream for a serving of frozen mango. By making these swaps gradually, you give your taste buds time to adjust and reduce the risk of feeling deprived or overwhelmed.

- Experiment with new cooking methods and flavors. Adopting an anti-inflammatory diet doesn't have to mean giving up on flavor and enjoyment. In fact, many anti-inflammatory foods are incredibly delicious when prepared in the right way. Try experimenting with new cooking methods, like roasting or grilling, or adding in new herbs and spices to boost the flavor of your meals. You may be surprised at how satisfying and delicious an anti-inflammatory diet can be.

- Make small changes to your meal timing and portion sizes. In addition to what you eat, how and when you eat can also have an impact on inflammation levels in the body. Try making small changes to your meal timing and portion sizes, like eating your largest meal earlier in the day or using smaller plates to help control portion sizes. Over time, these small shifts can add up to big improvements in your overall health and well-being.

The Importance of Patience and Self-Compassion

Of course, making even small changes to your diet and lifestyle can be challenging, especially when you're dealing with the pain and limitations of arthritis. It's important to approach the process with patience and self-compassion, recognizing that setbacks and slip-ups are a normal part of the journey.

When you do have a setback or struggle to stick to your goals, try to reframe it as a learning opportunity rather than a failure. What can you learn from the experience that can help you moving forward? Maybe you need to adjust your goals to be more realistic, or find new strategies for staying motivated and on track.

Most importantly, remember to be kind to yourself throughout the process. Adopting an anti-inflammatory diet is a journey, not a destination, and it's okay to take it one step at a time. By focusing on small, sustainable changes and treating yourself with compassion along the way, you can set yourself up for lasting success and a healthier, more vibrant life.

The Takeaway

Making the transition to an anti-inflammatory diet for managing arthritis can feel daunting, but it doesn't have to be an all-or-nothing proposition. By focusing on small, gradual changes over time, you can slowly but surely transform your diet and lifestyle in a way that feels sustainable and achievable.

6.2 Meal planning and preparation tips

Setting Yourself Up for Anti-Inflammatory Success

When it comes to adopting an anti-inflammatory diet for managing arthritis, a little planning and preparation can go a long way. By taking some time each week to plan out your meals and prep your ingredients, you can set yourself up for success and make the transition to a healthier way of eating feel more manageable and sustainable.

But let's face it – meal planning and preparation can feel overwhelming, especially if you're new to the process or dealing with the pain and limitations of arthritis. The good news is that with a few simple strategies and tools, you can streamline the process and make it work for your unique needs and lifestyle.

The Benefits of Meal Planning

So why is meal planning so important when it comes to adopting an anti-inflammatory diet? There are a few key reasons.

First, meal planning helps you stay on track with your goals. When you have a plan in place for what you're going to eat each day, you're less likely to make impulsive or unhealthy choices when hunger or cravings strike. Instead, you can rely on your pre-planned meals and snacks to keep you nourished and satisfied throughout the week.

Second, meal planning saves you time and energy in the long run. While it may take some extra effort upfront to plan out your meals and shop for ingredients, it can actually save you time and stress during the week when you're trying to juggle work, family, and other responsibilities. By having a plan in place, you can streamline your cooking and minimize the mental load of figuring out what to eat each day.

Finally, meal planning allows you to make the most of your anti-inflammatory ingredients. When you plan out your meals in advance, you can make sure you're incorporating a variety of anti-inflammatory foods into your diet and using up any perishable ingredients before they go bad. This can help you save money, reduce food waste, and ensure that you're getting the maximum benefit from your healthy eating efforts.

Tips for Effective Meal Planning

So how can you make meal planning work for you? Here are a few tips to get you started:

- Start with a template. Instead of starting from scratch each week, create a basic meal planning template that you can use as a starting point. This might include categories like breakfast, lunch, dinner, and snacks, as well as any specific dietary requirements or preferences you have.

- Make a master list of your favorite meals. Take some time to brainstorm a list of your favorite anti-inflammatory meals and snacks, including recipes you already know and love as well as new ones you'd like to try. Having a go-to list of meals can make the planning process feel less daunting and help you mix things up from week to week.

- Plan around your schedule. When planning out your meals for the week, be sure to take your schedule into account. If you know you have a busy day ahead, plan for a simple-prep meal or make extra portions of a recipe to have leftovers on hand. On days when you have more time, you can plan for more involved recipes or batch cooking sessions.

- Shop with a list. Once you have your meals planned out, make a shopping list of all the ingredients you'll need for the week. Be sure to check your pantry and fridge first to avoid buying duplicates, and organize your list by store section to make shopping more efficient.

- Prep ahead when possible. When you have some extra time, try to do some meal prep in advance to make the cooking process easier during the week. This might include washing and chopping vegetables, cooking grains or legumes, or even assembling entire meals that can be reheated later.

The Power of Batch Cooking

One of the most effective meal preparation strategies for an anti-inflammatory diet is batch cooking. Batch cooking involves preparing larger quantities of meals or ingredients ahead of time, which can then be portioned out and eaten throughout the week.

Batch cooking has several benefits for people with arthritis. First, it allows you to cook when you have the time and energy, rather than trying to prepare meals from scratch when you're feeling tired or in pain. Second, it ensures that you always have healthy, anti-inflammatory options on hand, even on days when cooking feels like too much of a challenge. Finally, it can save you money and reduce food waste by allowing you to buy ingredients in bulk and use up any leftovers.

Some examples of anti-inflammatory foods that work well for batch cooking include:
- Soups and stews
- Chilis and curries
- Grain salads and pilafs
- Roasted or grilled vegetables
- Baked or grilled proteins like chicken, fish, or tofu

When batch cooking, be sure to store your meals and ingredients properly to maximize their freshness and nutritional value. Use airtight containers and label them with the date and contents, and store them in the fridge or freezer as appropriate.

The Importance of Flexibility

While meal planning and preparation can be powerful tools for adopting an anti-inflammatory diet, it's important to remember that flexibility is key. Life happens, and there will be days when your carefully laid plans go out the window.

When this happens, try not to get discouraged or beat yourself up. Instead, focus on making the best choices you can in the moment, and get back on track with your next meal or the following day.

The Takeaway

Meal planning and preparation are essential tools for anyone looking to adopt an anti-inflammatory diet for managing arthritis. By taking some time each week to plan out your meals, shop for ingredients, and prep ahead when possible, you can set yourself up for success and make the transition to a healthier way of eating feel more manageable and sustainable.

6.3 Dining out and socializing on an anti-inflammatory diet

Navigating the Social Scene with Arthritis

When you're living with arthritis, the idea of dining out or socializing with friends and family can feel daunting. Will there be anything on the menu that fits with your anti-inflammatory diet? Will you be able to enjoy yourself without feeling deprived or left out? And what about those well-meaning loved ones who just don't seem to understand your dietary needs?

The good news is that with a little planning and communication, you can absolutely enjoy a vibrant social life while still staying true to your anti-inflammatory eating plan. Here are some tips and strategies to help you navigate the social scene with confidence and ease.

Doing Your Research

One of the most important things you can do when dining out on an anti-inflammatory diet is to do your research ahead of time. Take a few minutes to look up the menu of the restaurant you'll be visiting, either online or by calling ahead and asking for a copy.

As you scan the menu, look for dishes that are built around anti-inflammatory ingredients like colorful fruits and vegetables, whole grains, lean proteins, and healthy fats. Keep an eye out for any inflammatory ingredients that you're trying to avoid, like fried foods, processed meats, or dishes with a lot of added sugars or unhealthy fats.

If you don't see anything on the menu that fits with your dietary needs, don't be afraid to ask for modifications or substitutions. Many restaurants are happy to accommodate special requests, especially if you call ahead and give them some notice.

Communicating with Your Dining Companions

Another key to successfully dining out on an anti-inflammatory diet is communicating with your dining companions. Let them know ahead of time that you're following a specific eating plan to manage your arthritis symptoms, and that you may need to make some modifications to your order or bring your own food.

If you're worried about feeling left out or deprived, suggest a restaurant that has plenty of anti-inflammatory options on the menu, or offer to host a dinner party at your home where you can prepare dishes that everyone can enjoy.

Remember, your loved ones want to support you in your health journey, even if they don't always understand the specifics of your diet. By being open and honest about your needs and preferences, you can help create a dining experience that feels inclusive and enjoyable for everyone.

Navigating the Menu

When you're actually at the restaurant and looking at the menu, there are a few key things to keep in mind to help you make anti-inflammatory choices.

First, focus on dishes that are built around whole, minimally processed ingredients. Look for entrees that feature plenty of colorful fruits and vegetables, whole grains like quinoa or brown rice, and lean proteins like grilled chicken or fish.

If you're unsure about how a dish is prepared, don't be afraid to ask your server for more information. They should be able to tell you whether a dish contains any inflammatory ingredients or if it can be modified to fit your dietary needs.

When in doubt, opt for simple, straightforward dishes that you can easily customize. For example, a grilled fish or chicken entree with steamed vegetables and a side salad is a great option that can be easily modified to fit an anti-inflammatory diet.

Handling Social Pressure

One of the biggest challenges of dining out on an anti-inflammatory diet is dealing with social pressure from well-meaning friends and family. They may not understand why you're avoiding certain foods or may try to pressure you into indulging in something that doesn't fit with your eating plan.

In these situations, it's important to remember that your health is your top priority. You don't need to justify or explain your dietary choices to anyone, and you have the right to politely decline any food or drink that doesn't feel right for you.

If you're feeling particularly anxious or stressed about a social situation, it may be helpful to have a few polite but firm responses prepared ahead of time. For example, you might say something like, "Thank you so much for offering, but I'm following a specific eating plan to manage my arthritis symptoms and that doesn't work for me right now."

It can also be helpful to enlist the support of a close friend or family member who understands your dietary needs and can help run interference if needed. Having an ally by your side can make navigating social situations feel a lot less daunting.

Focusing on the Experience

Ultimately, dining out and socializing on an anti-inflammatory diet is about so much more than just the food on your plate. It's about connecting with loved ones, trying new experiences, and finding joy and pleasure in the moment.

Instead of getting hung up on what you can't eat or worrying about what others might think, try to focus on the overall experience of sharing a meal with people you care about. Savor the flavors and textures of the foods you can enjoy, engage in meaningful conversation, and let yourself be fully present in the moment.

Remember, adopting an anti-inflammatory diet is just one piece of the puzzle when it comes to managing your arthritis symptoms. It's important to also prioritize other lifestyle factors like regular exercise, stress management, and getting enough rest and sleep.

The Takeaway

Dining out and socializing on an anti-inflammatory diet can feel challenging at times, but it's absolutely possible to enjoy a vibrant social life while still staying true to your health goals. By doing your research, communicating with your dining companions, navigating the menu with care, and focusing on the overall experience, you can find joy and connection in any social situation.

6.4 Overcoming cravings and emotional eating

The Struggle is Real

Let's be real – adopting an anti-inflammatory diet for managing arthritis is no walk in the park. When you're used to eating a certain way, giving up your favorite comfort foods and go-to snacks can feel like a real challenge, especially when you're dealing with the pain and frustration of arthritis symptoms.

And then there are the cravings. Oh, the cravings. Whether it's a sudden urge for something salty, sweet, or deep-fried, cravings have a way of sneaking up on you when you least expect them, threatening to derail all your best intentions and hard work.

But here's the thing – cravings and emotional eating are a normal part of the human experience. They're not a sign of weakness or lack of willpower, and they certainly don't make you a bad person. In fact, by learning to recognize and manage your cravings in a healthy way, you can actually strengthen your relationship with food and your body, and find new ways to cope with the challenges of living with arthritis.

The Science of Cravings

So what exactly causes cravings, and why do they feel so darn hard to resist? Turns out, there are a few different factors at play.

First, there's the biological component. When we eat certain foods, especially those that are high in sugar, fat, or salt, our brains release feel-good chemicals like dopamine and serotonin. Over time, our brains start to associate those foods with pleasure and reward, creating a powerful drive to seek them out again and again.

There's also an emotional component to cravings. Many of us turn to food as a way to cope with stress, boredom, loneliness, or other difficult emotions. Eating can provide a temporary sense of comfort or distraction, even if it ultimately leaves us feeling worse in the long run.

Finally, there's the environmental factor. We live in a world that is constantly bombarding us with messages about food – from the billboards we pass on the highway to the commercials that interrupt our favorite TV shows. All of these messages can create a powerful pull towards certain foods, even if they don't align with our health goals.

Strategies for Managing Cravings

So how can you overcome cravings and emotional eating when you're trying to stick to an anti-inflammatory diet? Here are a few strategies to try:

- Practice mindfulness. When a craving hits, take a moment to pause and check in with yourself. What are you feeling in your body? What emotions are coming up for you? By bringing awareness to your experience, you can start to identify the underlying triggers for your cravings and find new ways to cope.
- Find healthy substitutes. If you're craving something sweet, try reaching for a piece of fruit or a small square of dark chocolate instead of a sugary snack. If you're in the mood for something salty, opt for a handful of nuts or some air-popped popcorn instead of chips.
- Distract yourself. Sometimes, simply getting your mind off the craving can be enough to make it pass. Try going for a walk, calling a friend, or engaging in a hobby or activity that you enjoy.
- Plan ahead. If you know that certain situations or emotions tend to trigger cravings for you, try to plan ahead and have healthy options on hand. Pack a nutritious snack for long car rides or keep a stash of herbal tea in your desk drawer for stressful days at work.
- Practice self-compassion. Remember, cravings and emotional eating are a normal part of the human experience. If you do give in to a craving, try not to beat yourself up about it. Instead, practice self-compassion and remind yourself that every moment is a new opportunity to make a different choice.

The Importance of Support

48

Overcoming cravings and emotional eating is no easy feat, especially when you're also dealing with the challenges of living with arthritis. That's why it's so important to have a strong support system in place as you navigate this journey.

Consider reaching out to a trusted friend, family member, or healthcare provider who can offer encouragement and accountability as you work to make changes to your diet and lifestyle. You might also consider joining a support group or online community of others who are living with arthritis and trying to adopt an anti-inflammatory diet.

Remember, you don't have to go through this alone. By surrounding yourself with people who understand and support your goals, you can find the strength and motivation to keep going, even when the cravings and emotions feel overwhelming.

Celebrating the Small Victories

Making changes to your diet and lifestyle is a journey, not a destination. It's not about perfection, but progress. And every small victory along the way is worth celebrating.

Maybe you went a whole day without giving in to a craving, or you found a new healthy recipe that you actually enjoyed. Maybe you had a difficult conversation with a loved one about your dietary needs, or you made it through a social event without feeling deprived or left out.

Whatever your small victories look like, take a moment to acknowledge and celebrate them. Give yourself credit for the hard work and dedication you're putting in, and remind yourself that every step forward is a step in the right direction.

The Takeaway

Overcoming cravings and emotional eating is a common challenge when adopting an anti-inflammatory diet for managing arthritis, but it's not an impossible one. By practicing mindfulness, finding healthy substitutes, planning ahead, and surrounding yourself with support, you can learn to manage your cravings in a way that feels empowering and sustainable.

Chapter 7: A 28-Day Anti-Inflammatory Meal Plan

7.1 Weekly meal plans with recipes and shopping lists

Day	Breakfast	Lunch	Dinner	Snack
1	Avocado Toast with Smoked Salmon	Grilled Chicken and Avocado Salad	Baked Salmon with Asparagus	Roasted Red Pepper Hummus
2	Quinoa Breakfast Bowl with Berries	Lentil and Vegetable Soup	Quinoa Stuffed Bell Peppers	Baked Zucchini Chips
3	Spinach and Feta Egg Muffins	Turkey and Hummus Wrap	Slow Cooker Beef and Vegetable Stew	Caprese Skewers
4	Overnight Chia Pudding with Mango	Tuna and White Bean Salad	Shrimp Stir-Fry with Vegetables	Guacamole
5	Sweet Potato Hash with Kale and Egg	Quinoa and Black Bean Burrito Bowl	Chickpea and Spinach Curry	Roasted Chickpeas
6	Banana Oatmeal Pancakes	Grilled Shrimp Skewers with Mango Salsa	Grilled Portobello Mushroom Burgers	Stuffed Cherry Tomatoes
7	Tofu Scramble with Vegetables	Mediterranean Tuna Salad	Baked Cod with Lemon and Herbs	Turkey and Avocado Roll-Ups
8	Blueberry Almond Smoothie Bowl	Veggie and Hummus Sandwich	Vegetable and Tofu Stir-Fry	Greek Yogurt Ranch Dip
9	Savory Oatmeal with Spinach and Mushrooms	Chicken and Quinoa Salad with Pesto	Lentil and Vegetable Soup	Watermelon and Feta Skewers
10	Greek Yogurt Parfait with Granola and Berries	Caprese Avocado Toast	Greek Chicken Pita Wraps	Peanut Butter and Banana Bites
11	Avocado and Egg Toast	Greek Yogurt Chicken Salad	Tuna and Avocado Salad	Cucumber and Hummus Bites
12	Peanut Butter and Banana Smoothie	Smoked Salmon and Cucumber Roll-Ups	Veggie and Hummus Wrap	Caprese Salad Skewers
13	Microwave Scrambled Eggs with Spinach	Vegetarian Burrito Bowl	Caprese Chicken Skillet	Baked Cinnamon Apples
14	Overnight Oats with Peanut Butter and Jelly	Tuna and Avocado Lettuce Wraps	Grilled Lemon Herb Chicken	Honey-Glazed Grilled Peaches

The above shopping list provides the necessary quantities of each ingredient to follow the 14-day meal plan for two people. Please note that the amounts listed have been calculated specifically to accommodate two individuals:

Fruits:

Avocados: 6

Bananas: 4

Berries (mixed): 3 cups

Blueberries: 1 1/2 cups

Lemon: 3

Limes: 2

Mango: 2

Peaches: 3

Vegetables:

Asparagus: 1 medium bunch

Bell peppers: 4

Cherry tomatoes: 1 1/2 pints

Cucumber: 3

Garlic: 1 medium head

Kale: 1 medium bunch

Mushrooms: 6 oz

Onions: 4

Portobello mushrooms: 3

Red onion: 2

Romaine lettuce: 2 heads

Spinach: 1 1/2 lbs

Sweet potatoes: 3

Tomatoes: 6

Zucchini: 3

Proteins:

Chicken breast: 4 lbs

Cod fillets: 1 1/2 lbs

Eggs: 1 1/2 dozen

Salmon fillets: 3 lbs

Shrimp: 1 1/2 lbs

Smoked salmon: 6 oz

Tofu: 1 1/2 lbs

Tuna (canned): 4 cans

Turkey breast (deli-sliced): 12 oz

Grains and Legumes:

Black beans (canned): 3 cans

Chickpeas (canned): 3 cans

Lentils (dry): 1 1/2 lbs

Oats: 1 1/2 lbs

Pita bread: 6

Quinoa: 1 1/2 lbs

Tortillas (whole wheat): 6

White beans (canned): 2 cans

Dairy and Alternatives:

Almond milk: 3/4 gallon

Feta cheese: 6 oz

Greek yogurt: 1 1/2 lbs

Hummus: 1 1/2 lbs

Peanut butter: 1 medium jar

Unsweetened almond milk: 3/4 gallon

Nuts and Seeds:

Almonds: 12 oz

Chia seeds: 12 oz

Peanuts: 12 oz

Walnuts: 12 oz

Herbs and Spices:

Basil: 1 medium bunch

Cinnamon: 1 medium jar

Cumin: 1 medium jar

Mint: 1 medium bunch

Oregano: 1 medium jar

Parsley: 1 medium bunch

Rosemary: 1 medium jar

Thyme: 1 medium jar

Turmeric: 1 medium jar

Oils and Vinegars:

Apple cider vinegar: 1 medium bottle

Balsamic vinegar: 1 medium bottle

Coconut oil: 1 medium jar

Olive oil: 1 medium bottle

Miscellaneous:

Almond butter: 1 medium jar

Granola: 1 medium bag

Honey: 1 medium jar

Salsa: 1 medium jar

Vanilla extract: 1 medium bottle

Part IV: The Recipes

Chapter 8: Rise & Shine Breakfasts

Avocado Toast with Smoked Salmon

PREPARATION TIME = 10 minutes

INGREDIENTS = 2 slices whole grain bread | 1 ripe avocado | 4 oz smoked salmon | 1/4 red onion, thinly sliced | 1 tbsp capers | Lemon juice to taste | Salt and pepper to taste

SERVINGS = Serves 2

MODE OF COOKING = Toaster

PROCEDURE =

Toast bread until crisp and golden.

Mash avocado with a fork and spread onto toast. Season with salt, pepper, and lemon juice.

Top with smoked salmon, red onion, and capers.

NUTRITIONAL VALUES = 350 calories | 20g protein | 20g fat | 25g carbohydrates | 8g fiber

Quinoa Breakfast Bowl with Berries [Vegan, Gluten-Free]

PREPARATION TIME = 20 minutes

INGREDIENTS = 1 cup quinoa | 2 cups water | 1 cup almond milk | 1 tsp cinnamon | 1 tbsp maple syrup | 1 cup mixed berries | 1/4 cup sliced almonds

SERVINGS = Serves 4

MODE OF COOKING = Stovetop

PROCEDURE =

Rinse quinoa thoroughly and drain.

In a pot, bring water to a boil. Add quinoa, reduce heat, and simmer for 15 minutes until tender.

Stir in almond milk, cinnamon, and maple syrup. Divide into bowls.

Top with mixed berries and sliced almonds.

NUTRITIONAL VALUES = 300 calories | 10g protein | 8g fat | 50g carbohydrates | 8g fiber

Spinach and Feta Egg Muffins [Vegetarian, Gluten-Free]

PREPARATION TIME = 30 minutes

INGREDIENTS = 6 eggs | 1 cup fresh spinach, chopped | 1/2 cup crumbled feta cheese | 1/4 cup diced onion | 1/4 cup diced red bell pepper | 1 tsp olive oil | Salt and pepper to taste

SERVINGS = Makes 12 muffins

MODE OF COOKING = Oven

PROCEDURE =

Preheat oven to 350°F (175°C). Grease a 12-cup muffin tin.

In a bowl, whisk eggs with salt and pepper.

In a skillet, heat olive oil over medium heat. Add onion and bell pepper, and cook until softened. Stir in spinach until wilted.

Divide vegetable mixture and feta cheese evenly among muffin cups. Pour egg mixture over the top.

Bake for 20-25 minutes, until set and lightly golden.

NUTRITIONAL VALUES = 100 calories | 7g protein | 7g fat | 2g carbohydrates | 1g fiber

Overnight Chia Pudding with Mango [Vegan, Gluten-Free, Lactose-Free]

PREPARATION TIME = 5 minutes (plus overnight chilling)

INGREDIENTS = 1/2 cup chia seeds | 2 cups coconut milk | 1 tsp vanilla extract | 1 tbsp maple syrup | 1 ripe mango, diced | 1/4 cup unsweetened shredded coconut

SERVINGS = Serves 4

MODE OF COOKING = No-cook

PROCEDURE =

In a jar or container, combine chia seeds, coconut milk, vanilla extract, and maple syrup. Stir well.

Cover and refrigerate overnight (or for at least 4 hours).

In the morning, divide into bowls and top with diced mango and shredded coconut.

NUTRITIONAL VALUES = 300 calories | 6g protein | 20g fat | 30g carbohydrates | 12g fiber

Sweet Potato Hash with Kale and Egg

PREPARATION TIME = 30 minutes

INGREDIENTS = 2 sweet potatoes, diced | 2 cups kale, chopped | 1/2 onion, diced | 2 cloves garlic, minced | 2 tbsp olive oil | 4 eggs | Salt and pepper to taste

SERVINGS = Serves 4

MODE OF COOKING = Stovetop

PROCEDURE =

In a large skillet, heat olive oil over medium heat. Add onion and garlic, and cook until softened.

Add sweet potatoes and cook for 10-15 minutes, stirring occasionally, until tender and lightly browned.

Stir in kale and cook until wilted. Season with salt and pepper.

Create 4 wells in the hash and crack an egg into each. Cover and cook until whites are set and yolks are runny.

NUTRITIONAL VALUES = 300 calories | 12g protein | 15g fat | 30g carbohydrates | 6g fiber

Banana Oatmeal Pancakes [Lactose-Free]

PREPARATION TIME = 20 minutes

INGREDIENTS = 2 ripe bananas | 2 eggs | 1 cup rolled oats | 1 tsp baking powder | 1 tsp vanilla extract | 1/2 tsp cinnamon | Coconut oil for cooking

SERVINGS = Makes 8 pancakes

MODE OF COOKING = Stovetop

PROCEDURE =

In a blender, combine bananas, eggs, oats, baking powder, vanilla extract, and cinnamon. Blend until smooth.

Heat a non-stick skillet over medium heat. Grease with coconut oil.

Spoon batter into rounds and cook for 2-3 minutes per side, until golden brown.

NUTRITIONAL VALUES = 150 calories | 5g protein | 5g fat | 20g carbohydrates | 3g fiber

Tofu Scramble with Vegetables [Vegan, Gluten-Free, Lactose-Free]

PREPARATION TIME = 20 minutes

INGREDIENTS = 1 block firm tofu, crumbled | 1 cup mixed vegetables (e.g., bell peppers, zucchini, mushrooms) | 1/2 onion, diced | 2 cloves garlic, minced | 1 tbsp olive oil | 1 tsp turmeric | Salt and pepper to taste

SERVINGS = Serves 4

MODE OF COOKING = Stovetop

PROCEDURE =

In a large skillet, heat olive oil over medium heat. Add onion and garlic, and cook until softened.

Add mixed vegetables and cook until tender-crisp.

Stir in crumbled tofu and turmeric. Season with salt and pepper. Cook for 5 minutes, stirring occasionally, until heated through.

NUTRITIONAL VALUES = 200 calories | 15g protein | 12g fat | 10g carbohydrates | 4g fiber

Blueberry Almond Smoothie Bowl [Gluten-Free]

PREPARATION TIME = 10 minutes

INGREDIENTS = 1 frozen banana | 1 cup frozen blueberries | 1 cup almond milk | 1 tbsp almond butter | 1 tsp honey | 1/4 cup granola | 1 tbsp sliced almonds

SERVINGS = Serves 1

MODE OF COOKING = Blender

PROCEDURE =

In a blender, combine frozen banana, blueberries, almond milk, almond butter, and honey. Blend until smooth.

Pour into a bowl and top with granola and sliced almonds.

NUTRITIONAL VALUES = 400 calories | 10g protein | 20g fat | 50g carbohydrates | 10g fiber

Savory Oatmeal with Spinach and Mushrooms [Vegan, Gluten-Free, Lactose-Free]

PREPARATION TIME = 20 minutes

INGREDIENTS = 1 cup rolled oats | 2 cups vegetable broth | 1 cup fresh spinach, chopped | 1 cup sliced mushrooms | 1/4 onion, diced | 1 clove garlic, minced | 1 tsp olive oil | Salt and pepper to taste

SERVINGS = Serves 2

MODE OF COOKING = Stovetop

PROCEDURE =

In a pot, bring vegetable broth to a boil. Add oats, reduce heat, and simmer for 10-15 minutes until tender.

In a skillet, heat olive oil over medium heat. Add onion and garlic, and cook until softened.

Add mushrooms and cook until tender. Stir in spinach until wilted.

Divide oatmeal into bowls and top with vegetable mixture. Season with salt and pepper.

NUTRITIONAL VALUES = 250 calories | 10g protein | 6g fat | 40g carbohydrates | 8g fiber

Greek Yogurt Parfait with Granola and Berries

PREPARATION TIME = 10 minutes

INGREDIENTS = 2 cups Greek yogurt | 1 cup granola | 1 cup mixed berries (e.g., strawberries, raspberries, blueberries) | 2 tbsp honey

SERVINGS = Serves 4

MODE OF COOKING = No-cook

PROCEDURE =

In glasses or jars, layer Greek yogurt, granola, and mixed berries.

Drizzle with honey and serve.

NUTRITIONAL VALUES = 250 calories | 15g protein | 8g fat | 30g carbohydrates | 4g fiber

Quick Recipes (Under 15 Minutes):

Avocado and Egg Toast

PREPARATION TIME = 10 minutes

INGREDIENTS = 2 slices whole grain bread | 1 ripe avocado | 2 eggs | 1 tsp olive oil | Salt and pepper to taste

SERVINGS = Serves 2

MODE OF COOKING = Toaster and Stovetop

PROCEDURE =

Toast bread until crisp and golden.

Mash avocado with a fork and spread onto toast. Season with salt and pepper.

In a skillet, heat olive oil over medium heat. Fry eggs until whites are set and yolks are runny.

Top avocado toast with fried eggs.

NUTRITIONAL VALUES = 300 calories | 15g protein | 20g fat | 20g carbohydrates | 6g fiber

---

Peanut Butter and Banana Smoothie [Gluten-Free]

PREPARATION TIME = 5 minutes

INGREDIENTS = 1 ripe banana | 1 cup almond milk | 2 tbsp peanut butter | 1 tsp honey | 1/2 tsp cinnamon

SERVINGS = Serves 1

MODE OF COOKING = Blender

PROCEDURE =

In a blender, combine banana, almond milk, peanut butter, honey, and cinnamon. Blend until smooth.

NUTRITIONAL VALUES = 350 calories | 12g protein | 20g fat | 35g carbohydrates | 6g fiber

---

Microwave Scrambled Eggs with Spinach

PREPARATION TIME = 5 minutes

INGREDIENTS = 2 eggs | 1/4 cup milk | 1/2 cup fresh spinach, chopped | Salt and pepper to taste

SERVINGS = Serves 1

MODE OF COOKING = Microwave

PROCEDURE =

In a microwave-safe bowl, whisk eggs with milk, salt, and pepper.

Stir in chopped spinach.

Microwave on high for 1-2 minutes, stirring every 30 seconds, until eggs are set.

NUTRITIONAL VALUES = 200 calories | 15g protein | 12g fat | 5g carbohydrates | 1g fiber

---

Overnight Oats with Peanut Butter and Jelly [Vegetarian, Gluten-Free]

PREPARATION TIME = 5 minutes (plus overnight chilling)

INGREDIENTS = 1/2 cup rolled oats | 1/2 cup almond milk | 2 tbsp peanut butter | 1 tbsp strawberry jam | 1/4 cup fresh strawberries, sliced

SERVINGS = Serves 1

MODE OF COOKING = No-cook

PROCEDURE =

In a jar or container, combine oats, almond milk, peanut butter, and jam. Stir well.

Cover and refrigerate overnight (or for at least 4 hours).

In the morning, top with sliced strawberries.

NUTRITIONAL VALUES = 400 calories | 15g protein | 20g fat | 45g carbohydrates | 8g fiber

Cottage Cheese with Tomatoes and Basil [Gluten-Free]

PREPARATION TIME = 5 minutes

INGREDIENTS = 1 cup cottage cheese | 1 cup cherry tomatoes, halved | 1/4 cup fresh basil leaves, torn | 1 tsp olive oil | Salt and pepper to taste

SERVINGS = Serves 1

MODE OF COOKING = No-cook

PROCEDURE =

In a bowl, combine cottage cheese, cherry tomatoes, basil leaves, olive oil, salt, and pepper. Gently toss until well mixed.

NUTRITIONAL VALUES = 250 calories | 25g protein | 10g fat | 15g carbohydrates | 2g fiber

Chapter 9: Lunches for Home or On-The-Go

Grilled Chicken and Avocado Salad [Meat]

PREPARATION TIME = 20 minutes

INGREDIENTS = 2 boneless, skinless chicken breasts | 1 ripe avocado, diced | 4 cups mixed greens | 1 cup cherry tomatoes, halved | 1/4 red onion, thinly sliced | 2 tbsp olive oil | 1 tbsp lemon juice | Salt and pepper to taste

SERVINGS = Serves 2

MODE OF COOKING = Grill or Stovetop

PROCEDURE =

Season chicken breasts with salt and pepper. Grill or cook in a skillet over medium heat until cooked through (165°F internal temperature).

In a large bowl, combine mixed greens, cherry tomatoes, red onion, and diced avocado.

Slice cooked chicken and add to the salad.

In a small bowl, whisk together olive oil, lemon juice, salt, and pepper. Drizzle over the salad and toss to combine.

NUTRITIONAL VALUES = 400 calories | 30g protein | 25g fat | 15g carbohydrates | 8g fiber

Baked Salmon with Quinoa and Roasted Vegetables [Fish]

PREPARATION TIME = 30 minutes

INGREDIENTS = 4 salmon fillets (4 oz each) | 1 cup quinoa | 2 cups water | 2 cups mixed vegetables (e.g., zucchini, bell peppers, red onion) | 2 tbsp olive oil | 1 tsp dried herbs (e.g., thyme, rosemary) | Salt and pepper to taste

SERVINGS = Serves 4

MODE OF COOKING = Oven

PROCEDURE =

Preheat oven to 400°F (200°C).

Rinse quinoa thoroughly and drain. In a pot, bring water to a boil. Add quinoa, reduce heat, and simmer for 15 minutes until tender.

On a baking sheet, toss mixed vegetables with 1 tbsp olive oil, salt, and pepper. Roast for 20 minutes.

Season salmon fillets with remaining olive oil, dried herbs, salt, and pepper. Place on a separate baking sheet and bake for 12-15 minutes, until easily flaked with a fork.

Divide quinoa and roasted vegetables among plates and top with baked salmon.

NUTRITIONAL VALUES = 450 calories | 30g protein | 20g fat | 35g carbohydrates | 6g fiber

Lentil and Vegetable Soup [Vegetarian]

PREPARATION TIME = 40 minutes

INGREDIENTS = 1 cup green or brown lentils | 4 cups vegetable broth | 1 onion, diced | 2 carrots, diced | 2 celery stalks, diced | 2 cloves garlic, minced | 1 cup diced tomatoes (canned or fresh) | 1 tsp cumin | 1 tsp paprika | 2 tbsp olive oil | Salt and pepper to taste

SERVINGS = Serves 4

MODE OF COOKING = Stovetop

PROCEDURE =

In a large pot, heat olive oil over medium heat. Add onion, carrots, celery, and garlic. Cook until softened.

Stir in lentils, vegetable broth, diced tomatoes, cumin, and paprika. Bring to a boil, then reduce heat and simmer for 25-30 minutes, until lentils are tender.

Season with salt and pepper to taste.

NUTRITIONAL VALUES = 300 calories | 15g protein | 8g fat | 45g carbohydrates | 15g fiber

Turkey and Hummus Wrap [Meat]

PREPARATION TIME = 10 minutes

INGREDIENTS = 2 whole wheat tortillas | 4 oz sliced turkey breast | 1/2 cup hummus | 1 cup mixed greens | 1/4 cucumber, thinly sliced | 1/4 red bell pepper, thinly sliced

SERVINGS = Serves 2

MODE OF COOKING = No-cook

PROCEDURE =

Spread hummus evenly over each tortilla.

Layer turkey, mixed greens, cucumber, and bell pepper on each tortilla.

Roll up tightly and slice in half.

NUTRITIONAL VALUES = 350 calories | 20g protein | 15g fat | 35g carbohydrates | 6g fiber

Tuna and White Bean Salad [Fish]

PREPARATION TIME = 15 minutes

INGREDIENTS = 1 can (5 oz) tuna in water, drained | 1 can (15 oz) white beans, drained and rinsed | 1 cup cherry tomatoes, halved | 1/4 red onion, thinly sliced | 2 tbsp olive oil | 1 tbsp lemon juice | Salt and pepper to taste

SERVINGS = Serves 2

MODE OF COOKING = No-cook

PROCEDURE =

In a large bowl, combine tuna, white beans, cherry tomatoes, and red onion.

In a small bowl, whisk together olive oil, lemon juice, salt, and pepper. Drizzle over the salad and toss to combine.

NUTRITIONAL VALUES = 400 calories | 25g protein | 15g fat | 40g carbohydrates | 10g fiber

Quinoa and Black Bean Burrito Bowl [Vegetarian]

PREPARATION TIME = 30 minutes

INGREDIENTS = 1 cup quinoa | 2 cups water | 1 can (15 oz) black beans, drained and rinsed | 1 cup corn kernels | 1 red bell pepper, diced | 1/4 red onion, diced | 1 avocado, diced | 2 tbsp olive oil | 1 tbsp lime juice | 1 tsp cumin | Salt and pepper to taste

SERVINGS = Serves 4

MODE OF COOKING = Stovetop

PROCEDURE =

Rinse quinoa thoroughly and drain. In a pot, bring water to a boil. Add quinoa, reduce heat, and simmer for 15 minutes until tender.

In a large bowl, combine cooked quinoa, black beans, corn, bell pepper, onion, and avocado.

In a small bowl, whisk together olive oil, lime juice, cumin, salt, and pepper. Drizzle over the quinoa mixture and toss to combine.

NUTRITIONAL VALUES = 400 calories | 15g protein | 20g fat | 50g carbohydrates | 12g fiber

Grilled Shrimp Skewers with Mango Salsa [Meat]

PREPARATION TIME = 25 minutes

INGREDIENTS = 1 lb large shrimp, peeled and deveined | 2 tbsp olive oil | 1 tsp chili powder | 1 mango, diced | 1 red bell pepper, diced | 1/4 red onion, diced | 1 jalapeño, seeded and minced | 1/4 cup fresh cilantro, chopped | 1 tbsp lime juice | Salt and pepper to taste

SERVINGS = Serves 4

MODE OF COOKING = Grill or Stovetop

PROCEDURE =

In a bowl, toss shrimp with olive oil, chili powder, salt, and pepper. Thread onto skewers.

Grill or cook shrimp skewers in a skillet over medium-high heat for 2-3 minutes per side, until pink and cooked through.

In a separate bowl, combine mango, bell pepper, onion, jalapeño, cilantro, lime juice, salt, and pepper to make the salsa.

Serve shrimp skewers topped with mango salsa.

NUTRITIONAL VALUES = 250 calories | 25g protein | 10g fat | 15g carbohydrates | 3g fiber

Mediterranean Tuna Salad [Fish]

PREPARATION TIME = 15 minutes

INGREDIENTS = 2 cans (5 oz each) tuna in olive oil, drained | 1 cup cherry tomatoes, halved | 1/2 cucumber, diced | 1/4 red onion, thinly sliced | 1/4 cup pitted Kalamata olives | 2 tbsp olive oil | 1 tbsp red wine vinegar | 1 tsp dried oregano | Salt and pepper to taste

SERVINGS = Serves 2

MODE OF COOKING = No-cook

PROCEDURE =

In a large bowl, combine tuna, cherry tomatoes, cucumber, red onion, and olives.

In a small bowl, whisk together olive oil, red wine vinegar, oregano, salt, and pepper. Drizzle over the salad and toss to combine.

NUTRITIONAL VALUES = 350 calories | 25g protein | 20g fat | 10g carbohydrates | 2g fiber

---

Veggie and Hummus Sandwich [Vegetarian]

PREPARATION TIME = 10 minutes

INGREDIENTS = 4 slices whole grain bread | 1/2 cup hummus | 1 avocado, mashed | 1 cucumber, thinly sliced | 1 tomato, thinly sliced | 1/4 red onion, thinly sliced | 1 cup alfalfa sprouts

SERVINGS = Serves 2

MODE OF COOKING = No-cook

PROCEDURE =

Spread hummus on two slices of bread and mashed avocado on the other two slices.

Layer cucumber, tomato, red onion, and alfalfa sprouts on top of the hummus.

Top with the avocado slices of bread and cut sandwiches in half.

NUTRITIONAL VALUES = 400 calories | 15g protein | 20g fat | 45g carbohydrates | 12g fiber

---

Chicken and Quinoa Salad with Pesto [Meat]

PREPARATION TIME = 25 minutes

INGREDIENTS = 2 boneless, skinless chicken breasts | 1 cup quinoa | 2 cups water | 2 cups mixed greens | 1 cup cherry tomatoes, halved | 1/4 red onion, thinly sliced | 1/4 cup basil pesto | 2 tbsp olive oil | Salt and pepper to taste

SERVINGS = Serves 2

MODE OF COOKING = Stovetop

PROCEDURE =

Season chicken breasts with salt and pepper. Cook in a skillet over medium heat until cooked through (165°F internal temperature). Slice into strips.

Rinse quinoa thoroughly and drain. In a pot, bring water to a boil. Add quinoa, reduce heat, and simmer for 15 minutes until tender.

In a large bowl, combine cooked quinoa, mixed greens, cherry tomatoes, red onion, and sliced chicken.

In a small bowl, whisk together basil pesto and olive oil. Drizzle over the salad and toss to combine.

NUTRITIONAL VALUES = 500 calories | 30g protein | 25g fat | 40g carbohydrates | 6g fiber

Quick and Easy Recipes (Under 15 Minutes):

Caprese Avocado Toast [Vegetarian]

PREPARATION TIME = 10 minutes

INGREDIENTS = 2 slices whole grain bread | 1 avocado, mashed | 1 tomato, sliced | 4 oz fresh mozzarella, sliced | 1/4 cup fresh basil leaves | 1 tbsp balsamic glaze | Salt and pepper to taste

SERVINGS = Serves 2

MODE OF COOKING = Toaster

PROCEDURE =

Toast bread until crisp and golden.

Spread mashed avocado onto each slice of toast.

Top with tomato, mozzarella, and basil leaves.

Drizzle with balsamic glaze and season with salt and pepper.

NUTRITIONAL VALUES = 400 calories | 15g protein | 25g fat | 30g carbohydrates | 8g fiber

Greek Yogurt Chicken Salad [Meat]

PREPARATION TIME = 10 minutes

INGREDIENTS = 1 cup cooked chicken breast, diced | 1/2 cup Greek yogurt | 1/4 cup diced cucumber | 1/4 cup diced red onion | 1 tbsp lemon juice | 1 tsp dried dill | Salt and pepper to taste

SERVINGS = Serves 2

MODE OF COOKING = No-cook

PROCEDURE =

In a bowl, combine diced chicken, Greek yogurt, cucumber, red onion, lemon juice, dill, salt, and pepper.

Mix well and serve with whole grain crackers or in a wrap.

NUTRITIONAL VALUES = 250 calories | 30g protein | 8g fat | 10g carbohydrates | 1g fiber

Smoked Salmon and Cucumber Roll-Ups [Fish]

PREPARATION TIME = 10 minutes

INGREDIENTS = 4 oz smoked salmon | 1 cucumber, thinly sliced lengthwise | 4 oz cream cheese, softened | 1 tbsp chopped fresh dill | 1 tbsp lemon juice

SERVINGS = Serves 2

MODE OF COOKING = No-cook

PROCEDURE =

In a bowl, mix cream cheese, dill, and lemon juice until well combined.

Spread a thin layer of the cream cheese mixture onto each cucumber slice.

Place a slice of smoked salmon on top of the cream cheese and roll up tightly.

NUTRITIONAL VALUES = 200 calories | 15g protein | 15g fat | 5g carbohydrates | 1g fiber

Vegetarian Burrito Bowl [Vegetarian]

PREPARATION TIME = 15 minutes

INGREDIENTS = 1 cup cooked brown rice | 1 can (15 oz) black beans, drained and rinsed | 1 avocado, diced | 1 tomato, diced | 1/4 red onion, diced | 1/4 cup fresh cilantro, chopped | 1 tbsp lime juice | Salt and pepper to taste

SERVINGS = Serves 2

MODE OF COOKING = Microwave

PROCEDURE =

In a microwave-safe bowl, heat brown rice and black beans until warm.

Divide rice and beans between two bowls. Top with avocado, tomato, red onion, and cilantro.

Drizzle with lime juice and season with salt and pepper.

NUTRITIONAL VALUES = 400 calories | 15g protein | 15g fat | 60g carbohydrates | 15g fiber

Tuna and Avocado Lettuce Wraps [Fish]

PREPARATION TIME = 10 minutes

INGREDIENTS = 1 can (5 oz) tuna in water, drained | 1 avocado, mashed | 1 tbsp lemon juice | 1/4 cup diced red bell pepper | 8 large lettuce leaves | Salt and pepper to taste

SERVINGS = Serves 2

MODE OF COOKING = No-cook

PROCEDURE =

In a bowl, mix tuna, mashed avocado, lemon juice, bell pepper, salt, and pepper until well combined.

Spoon the mixture into the center of each lettuce leaf and roll up tightly.

NUTRITIONAL VALUES = 250 calories | 20g protein | 15g fat | 10g carbohydrates | 6g fiber

Chapter 10: Satisfying Soups and Salads

Chicken and Vegetable Soup [Meat]

PREPARATION TIME = 40 minutes

INGREDIENTS = 1 lb boneless, skinless chicken breast | 2 carrots, diced | 2 celery stalks, diced | 1 onion, diced | 2 cloves garlic, minced | 1 cup green beans, trimmed and cut | 1 cup diced tomatoes (canned or fresh) | 6 cups chicken broth | 1 tsp dried thyme | 2 tbsp olive oil | Salt and pepper to taste

SERVINGS = Serves 6

MODE OF COOKING = Stovetop

PROCEDURE =

In a large pot, heat olive oil over medium heat. Add onion, carrots, celery, and garlic. Cook until softened.

Add chicken breast, chicken broth, diced tomatoes, green beans, thyme, salt, and pepper. Bring to a boil, then reduce heat and simmer for 25-30 minutes.

Remove chicken breast, shred with two forks, and return to the soup. Serve hot.

NUTRITIONAL VALUES = 200 calories | 20g protein | 8g fat | 10g carbohydrates | 3g fiber

Salmon and Kale Salad [Fish]

PREPARATION TIME = 25 minutes

INGREDIENTS = 2 salmon fillets (4 oz each) | 4 cups kale, stemmed and chopped | 1 avocado, diced | 1/2 cup cherry tomatoes, halved | 1/4 red onion, thinly sliced | 2 tbsp olive oil | 1 tbsp lemon juice | Salt and pepper to taste

SERVINGS = Serves 2

MODE OF COOKING = Stovetop

PROCEDURE =

Season salmon fillets with salt and pepper. Cook in a skillet over medium heat for 4-5 minutes per side, until easily flaked with a fork.

In a large bowl, massage kale with 1 tbsp olive oil until softened.

Add avocado, cherry tomatoes, red onion, lemon juice, remaining olive oil, salt, and pepper to the kale. Toss to combine.

Divide salad between two plates and top with cooked salmon.

NUTRITIONAL VALUES = 450 calories | 30g protein | 30g fat | 15g carbohydrates | 6g fiber

Butternut Squash and Lentil Soup [Vegetarian]

PREPARATION TIME = 50 minutes

INGREDIENTS = 1 butternut squash, peeled, seeded, and cubed | 1 cup red lentils | 1 onion, diced | 2 cloves garlic, minced | 1 tsp ground cumin | 1 tsp ground turmeric | 1 tsp ground ginger | 4 cups vegetable broth | 1 can (13.5 oz) coconut milk | 2 tbsp olive oil | Salt and pepper to taste

SERVINGS = Serves 6

MODE OF COOKING = Stovetop

PROCEDURE =

In a large pot, heat olive oil over medium heat. Add onion and garlic. Cook until softened.

Add butternut squash, lentils, cumin, turmeric, ginger, vegetable broth, salt, and pepper. Bring to a boil, then reduce heat and simmer for 30-35 minutes, until squash and lentils are tender.

Stir in coconut milk and simmer for an additional 5 minutes. Serve hot.

NUTRITIONAL VALUES = 300 calories | 10g protein | 15g fat | 35g carbohydrates | 10g fiber

Turkey and Spinach Salad [Meat]

PREPARATION TIME = 20 minutes

INGREDIENTS = 8 oz sliced turkey breast | 4 cups baby spinach | 1/2 cup dried cranberries | 1/2 cup walnuts, chopped | 1/4 red onion, thinly sliced | 2 tbsp olive oil | 1 tbsp balsamic vinegar | Salt and pepper to taste

SERVINGS = Serves 2

MODE OF COOKING = No-cook

PROCEDURE =

In a large bowl, combine baby spinach, dried cranberries, walnuts, and red onion.

In a small bowl, whisk together olive oil, balsamic vinegar, salt, and pepper. Drizzle over the salad and toss to combine.

Divide salad between two plates and top with sliced turkey breast.

NUTRITIONAL VALUES = 400 calories | 25g protein | 25g fat | 20g carbohydrates | 5g fiber

Shrimp and Avocado Salad [Fish]

PREPARATION TIME = 20 minutes

INGREDIENTS = 1 lb large shrimp, peeled and deveined | 2 avocados, diced | 1 cucumber, diced | 1/4 red onion, thinly sliced | 1/4 cup fresh cilantro, chopped | 2 tbsp olive oil | 1 tbsp lime juice | Salt and pepper to taste

SERVINGS = Serves 4

MODE OF COOKING = Stovetop

PROCEDURE =

In a skillet, heat olive oil over medium heat. Cook shrimp for 2-3 minutes per side, until pink and cooked through.

In a large bowl, combine cooked shrimp, avocado, cucumber, red onion, cilantro, lime juice, salt, and pepper. Toss gently to combine.

NUTRITIONAL VALUES = 300 calories | 20g protein | 20g fat | 10g carbohydrates | 6g fiber

Roasted Red Pepper and Tomato Soup [Vegetarian]

PREPARATION TIME = 40 minutes

INGREDIENTS = 4 red bell peppers, roasted, peeled, and seeded | 4 tomatoes, roasted | 1 onion, diced | 2 cloves garlic, minced | 2 cups vegetable broth | 1 tsp dried basil | 1 tsp dried oregano | 2 tbsp olive oil | Salt and pepper to taste

SERVINGS = Serves 4

MODE OF COOKING = Stovetop

PROCEDURE =

Preheat oven to 450°F (230°C). Place whole bell peppers and tomatoes on a baking sheet and roast for 20-25 minutes, until charred.

Remove from oven, let cool slightly, then peel and seed peppers and tomatoes.

In a large pot, heat olive oil over medium heat. Add onion and garlic. Cook until softened.

Add roasted peppers, tomatoes, vegetable broth, basil, oregano, salt, and pepper. Bring to a boil, then reduce heat and simmer for 15 minutes.

Using an immersion blender or regular blender, puree the soup until smooth. Serve hot.

NUTRITIONAL VALUES = 150 calories | 3g protein | 10g fat | 15g carbohydrates | 4g fiber

Quinoa and Black Bean Salad [Vegetarian]

PREPARATION TIME = 30 minutes

INGREDIENTS = 1 cup quinoa | 2 cups water | 1 can (15 oz) black beans, drained and rinsed | 1 red bell pepper, diced | 1/4 red onion, diced | 1/4 cup fresh cilantro, chopped | 2 tbsp olive oil | 1 tbsp lime juice | 1 tsp ground cumin | Salt and pepper to taste

SERVINGS = Serves 4

MODE OF COOKING = Stovetop

PROCEDURE =

Rinse quinoa thoroughly and drain. In a pot, bring water to a boil. Add quinoa, reduce heat, and simmer for 15 minutes until tender.

In a large bowl, combine cooked quinoa, black beans, bell pepper, onion, and cilantro.

In a small bowl, whisk together olive oil, lime juice, cumin, salt, and pepper. Drizzle over the quinoa mixture and toss to combine.

NUTRITIONAL VALUES = 300 calories | 12g protein | 10g fat | 45g carbohydrates | 10g fiber

Chicken and Avocado Soup [Meat]

PREPARATION TIME = 40 minutes

INGREDIENTS = 1 lb boneless, skinless chicken breast | 2 avocados, diced | 1 onion, diced | 2 cloves garlic, minced | 1 jalapeño, seeded and minced | 6 cups chicken broth | 1/4 cup fresh

66

cilantro, chopped | 2 tbsp olive oil | 1 tbsp lime juice | Salt and pepper to taste

SERVINGS = Serves 6

MODE OF COOKING = Stovetop

PROCEDURE =

In a large pot, heat olive oil over medium heat. Add onion, garlic, and jalapeño. Cook until softened.

Add chicken breast, chicken broth, salt, and pepper. Bring to a boil, then reduce heat and simmer for 25-30 minutes.

Remove chicken breast, shred with two forks, and return to the soup.

Stir in avocado, cilantro, and lime juice. Serve hot.

NUTRITIONAL VALUES = 250 calories | 20g protein | 15g fat | 10g carbohydrates | 5g fiber

Tuna Niçoise Salad [Fish]

PREPARATION TIME = 30 minutes

INGREDIENTS = 2 cans (5 oz each) tuna in olive oil, drained | 4 cups mixed greens | 1 cup cherry tomatoes, halved | 1/2 cucumber, sliced | 1/4 red onion, thinly sliced | 1/4 cup pitted Kalamata olives | 2 hard-boiled eggs, quartered | 2 tbsp olive oil | 1 tbsp red wine vinegar | 1 tsp Dijon mustard | Salt and pepper to taste

SERVINGS = Serves 2

MODE OF COOKING = No-cook

PROCEDURE =

In a large bowl, combine mixed greens, cherry tomatoes, cucumber, red onion, and olives.

In a small bowl, whisk together olive oil, red wine vinegar, Dijon mustard, salt, and pepper. Drizzle over the salad and toss to combine.

Divide salad between two plates. Top with tuna and hard-boiled egg quarters.

NUTRITIONAL VALUES = 400 calories | 30g protein | 25g fat | 10g carbohydrates | 3g fiber

Carrot Ginger Soup [Vegetarian]

PREPARATION TIME = 40 minutes

INGREDIENTS = 1 lb carrots, peeled and chopped | 1 onion, diced | 2 cloves garlic, minced | 1 tbsp grated fresh ginger | 4 cups vegetable broth | 1 can (13.5 oz) coconut milk | 2 tbsp olive oil | Salt and pepper to taste

SERVINGS = Serves 4

MODE OF COOKING = Stovetop

PROCEDURE =

In a large pot, heat olive oil over medium heat. Add onion and garlic. Cook until softened.

Add carrots, ginger, vegetable broth, salt, and pepper. Bring to a boil, then reduce heat and simmer for 25-30 minutes, until carrots are tender.

Using an immersion blender or regular blender, puree the soup until smooth.

Stir in coconut milk and simmer for an additional 5 minutes. Serve hot.

NUTRITIONAL VALUES = 250 calories | 3g protein | 20g fat | 20g carbohydrates | 5g fiber

Quick and Easy Recipes (Under 15 Minutes):

Spinach and Strawberry Salad [Vegetarian]

PREPARATION TIME = 10 minutes

INGREDIENTS = 4 cups baby spinach | 1 cup sliced strawberries | 1/4 cup crumbled feta cheese | 1/4 cup sliced almonds | 2 tbsp olive oil | 1 tbsp balsamic vinegar | Salt and pepper to taste

SERVINGS = Serves 2

MODE OF COOKING = No-cook

PROCEDURE =

In a large bowl, combine baby spinach, strawberries, feta cheese, and sliced almonds.

In a small bowl, whisk together olive oil, balsamic vinegar, salt, and pepper. Drizzle over the salad and toss to combine.

NUTRITIONAL VALUES = 250 calories | 6g protein | 20g fat | 15g carbohydrates | 4g fiber

Tomato Basil Soup [Vegetarian]

PREPARATION TIME = 15 minutes

INGREDIENTS = 1 can (28 oz) diced tomatoes | 1 cup vegetable broth | 1/2 onion, diced | 2 cloves garlic, minced | 1/4 cup fresh basil, chopped | 1 tbsp olive oil | Salt and pepper to taste

SERVINGS = Serves 2

MODE OF COOKING = Stovetop

PROCEDURE =

In a pot, heat olive oil over medium heat. Add onion and garlic. Cook until softened.

Add diced tomatoes (with juice), vegetable broth, salt, and pepper. Bring to a boil, then reduce heat and simmer for 10 minutes.

Using an immersion blender or regular blender, puree the soup until smooth.

Stir in chopped basil and serve hot.

NUTRITIONAL VALUES = 150 calories | 3g protein | 7g fat | 20g carbohydrates | 5g fiber

Caprese Salad [Vegetarian]

PREPARATION TIME = 10 minutes

INGREDIENTS = 2 tomatoes, sliced | 8 oz fresh mozzarella, sliced | 1/4 cup fresh basil leaves | 2 tbsp olive oil | 1 tbsp balsamic vinegar | Salt and pepper to taste

SERVINGS = Serves 2

MODE OF COOKING = No-cook

PROCEDURE =

Arrange tomato and mozzarella slices on a plate, alternating between the two.

Scatter basil leaves over the top.

Drizzle with olive oil and balsamic vinegar. Season with salt and pepper.

NUTRITIONAL VALUES = 300 calories | 15g protein | 25g fat | 5g carbohydrates | 1g fiber

Cucumber and Avocado Soup [Vegetarian]

PREPARATION TIME = 10 minutes

INGREDIENTS = 2 cucumbers, peeled and chopped | 1 avocado, pitted and peeled | 1/2 cup Greek yogurt | 1/4 cup fresh dill, chopped | 1 tbsp lemon juice | Salt and pepper to taste

SERVINGS = Serves 2

MODE OF COOKING = Blender

PROCEDURE =

In a blender, combine cucumbers, avocado, Greek yogurt, dill, lemon juice, salt, and pepper. Blend until smooth.

Chill in the refrigerator for at least 30 minutes before serving.

NUTRITIONAL VALUES = 200 calories | 6g protein | 15g fat | 15g carbohydrates | 6g fiber

Watermelon and Feta Salad [Vegetarian]

PREPARATION TIME = 10 minutes

INGREDIENTS = 4 cups cubed watermelon | 1/2 cup crumbled feta cheese | 1/4 cup fresh mint leaves, chopped | 2 tbsp olive oil | 1 tbsp lime juice | Salt and pepper to taste

SERVINGS = Serves 4

MODE OF COOKING = No-cook

PROCEDURE =

In a large bowl, combine cubed watermelon, crumbled feta cheese, and chopped mint leaves.

In a small bowl, whisk together olive oil, lime juice, salt, and pepper. Drizzle over the salad and toss gently to combine.

NUTRITIONAL VALUES = 150 calories | 4g protein | 10g fat | 15g carbohydrates | 1g fiber

Chapter 11: Delicious Dinners

Grilled Lemon Herb Chicken [Meat]

PREPARATION TIME = 30 minutes (plus marinating time)

INGREDIENTS = 4 boneless, skinless chicken breasts | 1/4 cup olive oil | 1/4 cup lemon juice | 2 cloves garlic, minced | 1 tsp dried oregano | 1 tsp dried basil | Salt and pepper to taste

SERVINGS = Serves 4

MODE OF COOKING = Grill or Stovetop

PROCEDURE =

In a bowl, whisk together olive oil, lemon juice, garlic, oregano, basil, salt, and pepper.

Place chicken breasts in a shallow dish and pour marinade over the top. Cover and refrigerate for at least 30 minutes, or up to 2 hours.

Preheat grill or grill pan to medium-high heat. Remove chicken from marinade and discard remaining marinade.

Grill chicken for 6-8 minutes per side, until cooked through (165°F internal temperature). Serve hot.

NUTRITIONAL VALUES = 250 calories | 30g protein | 15g fat | 2g carbohydrates | 0g fiber

Baked Salmon with Asparagus [Fish]

PREPARATION TIME = 25 minutes

INGREDIENTS = 4 salmon fillets (4 oz each) | 1 bunch asparagus, trimmed | 2 tbsp olive oil | 1 tbsp lemon juice | 2 cloves garlic, minced | Salt and pepper to taste

SERVINGS = Serves 4

MODE OF COOKING = Oven

PROCEDURE =

Preheat oven to 400°F (200°C).

Arrange salmon fillets and asparagus on a baking sheet. Drizzle with olive oil and lemon juice, then sprinkle with garlic, salt, and pepper.

Bake for 12-15 minutes, until salmon is easily flaked with a fork and asparagus is tender.

NUTRITIONAL VALUES = 300 calories | 25g protein | 20g fat | 5g carbohydrates | 2g fiber

Quinoa Stuffed Bell Peppers [Vegetarian]

PREPARATION TIME = 40 minutes

INGREDIENTS = 4 bell peppers, halved and seeded | 1 cup quinoa | 2 cups vegetable broth | 1 can (15 oz) black beans, drained and rinsed | 1 tomato, diced | 1/4 onion, diced | 2 cloves garlic, minced | 1 tsp ground cumin | 1 tsp chili powder | 1/4 cup fresh cilantro, chopped | Salt and pepper to taste

SERVINGS = Serves 4

MODE OF COOKING = Stovetop and Oven

PROCEDURE =

Preheat oven to 375°F (190°C).

Rinse quinoa thoroughly and drain. In a pot, bring vegetable broth to a boil. Add quinoa, reduce heat, and simmer for 15 minutes until tender.

In a large bowl, combine cooked quinoa, black beans, tomato, onion, garlic, cumin, chili powder, cilantro, salt, and pepper.

Spoon quinoa mixture into bell pepper halves and place on a baking sheet.

Bake for 20-25 minutes, until peppers are tender.

NUTRITIONAL VALUES = 300 calories | 15g protein | 5g fat | 50g carbohydrates | 12g fiber

Slow Cooker Beef and Vegetable Stew [Meat]

PREPARATION TIME = 20 minutes (plus 6-8 hours cooking time)

INGREDIENTS = 1 lb beef stew meat, cut into 1-inch cubes | 2 carrots, chopped | 2 celery stalks, chopped | 1 onion, chopped | 2 potatoes, peeled and cubed | 2 cloves garlic, minced | 1 can (14.5 oz) diced tomatoes | 2 cups beef broth | 1 tsp dried thyme | 1 tsp dried rosemary | 2 tbsp olive oil | Salt and pepper to taste

SERVINGS = Serves 6

MODE OF COOKING = Slow Cooker

PROCEDURE =

In a large skillet, heat olive oil over medium-high heat. Add beef cubes and cook until browned on all sides.

Transfer beef to a slow cooker. Add carrots, celery, onion, potatoes, garlic, diced tomatoes (with juice), beef broth, thyme, rosemary, salt, and pepper.

Cover and cook on low for 6-8 hours, until beef and vegetables are tender.

NUTRITIONAL VALUES = 300 calories | 25g protein | 12g fat | 20g carbohydrates | 4g fiber

Shrimp Stir-Fry with Vegetables [Fish]

PREPARATION TIME = 25 minutes

INGREDIENTS = 1 lb large shrimp, peeled and deveined | 2 cups mixed vegetables (e.g., bell peppers, zucchini, carrots) | 1 onion, sliced | 2 cloves garlic, minced | 1 tbsp grated fresh ginger | 2 tbsp olive oil | 2 tbsp soy sauce (low-sodium) | 1 tbsp rice vinegar | 1 tsp sesame oil | Salt and pepper to taste

SERVINGS = Serves 4

MODE OF COOKING = Stovetop

PROCEDURE =

In a wok or large skillet, heat olive oil over medium-high heat. Add onion, garlic, and ginger. Stir-fry for 1-2 minutes.

Add mixed vegetables and stir-fry for 3-4 minutes, until tender-crisp.

Add shrimp and stir-fry for 2-3 minutes, until pink and cooked through.

In a small bowl, whisk together soy sauce, rice vinegar, and sesame oil. Pour over the stir-fry and toss to combine. Season with salt and pepper.

Serve hot, with brown rice if desired.

NUTRITIONAL VALUES = 250 calories | 25g protein | 10g fat | 15g carbohydrates | 4g fiber

Chickpea and Spinach Curry [Vegetarian]

PREPARATION TIME = 30 minutes

INGREDIENTS = 1 can (15 oz) chickpeas, drained and rinsed | 1 can (14.5 oz) diced tomatoes | 1 onion, diced | 2 cloves garlic, minced | 1 tbsp grated fresh ginger | 2 cups fresh spinach | 1 tbsp olive oil | 1 tbsp curry powder | 1 tsp ground cumin | 1 tsp ground turmeric | 1 cup vegetable broth | Salt and pepper to taste

SERVINGS = Serves 4

MODE OF COOKING = Stovetop

PROCEDURE =

In a large pot, heat olive oil over medium heat. Add onion, garlic, and ginger. Cook until softened.

Stir in curry powder, cumin, and turmeric. Cook for 1-2 minutes, until fragrant.

Add chickpeas, diced tomatoes (with juice), vegetable broth, salt, and pepper. Bring to a boil, then reduce heat and simmer for 15 minutes.

Stir in spinach and cook until wilted. Serve hot, with brown rice if desired.

NUTRITIONAL VALUES = 250 calories | 10g protein | 8g fat | 35g carbohydrates | 10g fiber

Grilled Portobello Mushroom Burgers [Vegetarian]

PREPARATION TIME = 25 minutes

INGREDIENTS = 4 large portobello mushroom caps | 1/4 cup olive oil | 2 tbsp balsamic vinegar | 2 cloves garlic, minced | 1 tsp dried basil | 1 tsp dried oregano | 4 whole wheat buns | 1 tomato, sliced | 1/4 red onion, sliced | Salt and pepper to taste

SERVINGS = Serves 4

MODE OF COOKING = Grill or Stovetop

PROCEDURE =

In a bowl, whisk together olive oil, balsamic vinegar, garlic, basil, oregano, salt, and pepper.

Place mushroom caps in a shallow dish and pour marinade over the top. Let marinate for 10-15 minutes.

Preheat grill or grill pan to medium-high heat. Remove mushrooms from marinade and discard remaining marinade.

Grill mushrooms for 4-5 minutes per side, until tender.

Serve mushrooms on whole wheat buns, topped with tomato and red onion slices.

NUTRITIONAL VALUES = 300 calories | 8g protein | 20g fat | 25g carbohydrates | 5g fiber

Baked Cod with Lemon and Herbs [Fish]

PREPARATION TIME = 25 minutes

INGREDIENTS = 4 cod fillets (4 oz each) | 2 tbsp olive oil | 2 tbsp lemon juice | 2 cloves garlic, minced | 1 tsp dried parsley | 1 tsp dried dill | Salt and pepper to taste

SERVINGS = Serves 4

MODE OF COOKING = Oven

PROCEDURE =

Preheat oven to 400°F (200°C).

Arrange cod fillets in a baking dish. Drizzle with olive oil and lemon juice, then sprinkle with garlic, parsley, dill, salt, and pepper.

Bake for 10-12 minutes, until fish is easily flaked with a fork.

NUTRITIONAL VALUES = 200 calories | 25g protein | 10g fat | 2g carbohydrates | 0g fiber

(low-sodium) | 1 tbsp rice vinegar | 1 tsp sesame oil | Salt and pepper to taste

SERVINGS = Serves 4

MODE OF COOKING = Stovetop

PROCEDURE =

In a wok or large skillet, heat olive oil over medium-high heat. Add onion, garlic, and ginger. Stir-fry for 1-2 minutes.

Add mixed vegetables and stir-fry for 3-4 minutes, until tender-crisp.

Add tofu and stir-fry for 2-3 minutes, until heated through.

In a small bowl, whisk together soy sauce, rice vinegar, and sesame oil. Pour over the stir-fry and toss to combine. Season with salt and pepper.

Serve hot, with brown rice if desired.

NUTRITIONAL VALUES = 250 calories | 15g protein | 15g fat | 15g carbohydrates | 5g fiber

Vegetable and Tofu Stir-Fry [Vegetarian]

PREPARATION TIME = 25 minutes

INGREDIENTS = 1 block (14 oz) firm tofu, drained and cubed | 2 cups mixed vegetables (e.g., broccoli, carrots, bell peppers) | 1 onion, sliced | 2 cloves garlic, minced | 1 tbsp grated fresh ginger | 2 tbsp olive oil | 2 tbsp soy sauce

Lentil and Vegetable Soup [Vegetarian]

PREPARATION TIME = 40 minutes

INGREDIENTS = 1 cup green or brown lentils | 4 cups vegetable broth | 1 onion, diced | 2 carrots, diced | 2 celery stalks, diced | 2 cloves garlic, minced | 1 can (14.5 oz) diced tomatoes | 1 tsp ground cumin | 1 tsp dried thyme | 2 tbsp olive oil | Salt and pepper to taste

SERVINGS = Serves 4

MODE OF COOKING = Stovetop

PROCEDURE =

In a large pot, heat olive oil over medium heat. Add onion, carrots, celery, and garlic. Cook until softened.

Stir in lentils, vegetable broth, diced tomatoes, cumin, thyme, salt, and pepper. Bring to a boil, then reduce heat and simmer for 25-30 minutes, until lentils are tender.

Serve hot, with a slice of whole grain bread if desired.

NUTRITIONAL VALUES = 300 calories | 15g protein | 8g fat | 45g carbohydrates | 15g fiber

Quick and Easy Recipes (Under 30 Minutes):

Greek Chicken Pita Wraps [Meat]

PREPARATION TIME = 20 minutes

INGREDIENTS = 2 boneless, skinless chicken breasts, sliced | 1 tbsp olive oil | 1 tsp dried oregano | 4 whole wheat pitas | 1 tomato, diced | 1/2 cucumber, diced | 1/4 red onion, diced | 1/4 cup crumbled feta cheese | 2 tbsp tzatziki sauce | Salt and pepper to taste

SERVINGS = Serves 4

MODE OF COOKING = Stovetop

PROCEDURE =

In a skillet, heat olive oil over medium-high heat. Add sliced chicken, oregano, salt, and pepper. Cook for 5-7 minutes, until chicken is cooked through.

Warm pitas in the microwave or on a griddle.

Divide chicken, tomato, cucumber, red onion, and feta cheese among the pitas.

Drizzle with tzatziki sauce and wrap tightly.

NUTRITIONAL VALUES = 350 calories | 25g protein | 12g fat | 35g carbohydrates | 5g fiber

Tuna and Avocado Salad [Fish]

PREPARATION TIME = 15 minutes

INGREDIENTS = 2 cans (5 oz each) tuna in water, drained | 1 avocado, diced | 1/4 red onion, diced | 1 tbsp lemon juice | 2 tbsp olive oil | Salt and pepper to taste | 4 cups mixed greens

SERVINGS = Serves 2

MODE OF COOKING = No-cook

PROCEDURE =

In a bowl, combine tuna, avocado, red onion, lemon juice, olive oil, salt, and pepper. Mix gently.

Serve over a bed of mixed greens.

NUTRITIONAL VALUES = 350 calories | 25g protein | 20g fat | 10g carbohydrates | 5g fiber

Veggie and Hummus Wrap [Vegetarian]

PREPARATION TIME = 10 minutes

INGREDIENTS = 2 whole wheat tortillas | 1/2 cup hummus | 1 cucumber, sliced | 1 red bell pepper, sliced | 1/4 red onion, sliced | 1 cup alfalfa sprouts

SERVINGS = Serves 2

MODE OF COOKING = No-cook

PROCEDURE =

Spread hummus evenly over each tortilla.

Layer cucumber, bell pepper, red onion, and alfalfa sprouts on each tortilla.

Roll up tightly and cut in half.

NUTRITIONAL VALUES = 300 calories | 10g protein | 12g fat | 40g carbohydrates | 8g fiber

---

Caprese Chicken Skillet [Meat]

PREPARATION TIME = 25 minutes

INGREDIENTS = 4 boneless, skinless chicken breasts | 1 tbsp olive oil | 1 tomato, sliced | 4 oz fresh mozzarella, sliced | 1/4 cup fresh basil leaves | 2 tbsp balsamic vinegar | Salt and pepper to taste

SERVINGS = Serves 4

MODE OF COOKING = Stovetop

PROCEDURE =

Season chicken breasts with salt and pepper.

In a large skillet, heat olive oil over medium-high heat. Add chicken and cook for 6-8 minutes per side, until cooked through.

Top each chicken breast with a slice of tomato and a slice of mozzarella. Cover skillet and cook for 1-2 minutes, until cheese is melted.

Drizzle with balsamic vinegar and garnish with fresh basil leaves.

NUTRITIONAL VALUES = 300 calories | 35g protein | 15g fat | 5g carbohydrates | 1g fibe

Chapter 12: Snacks and Appetizers

Spinach and Artichoke Dip [Vegetarian]

PREPARATION TIME = 30 minutes

INGREDIENTS = 1 cup frozen spinach, thawed and chopped | 1 can (14 oz) artichoke hearts, drained and chopped | 1/2 cup Greek yogurt | 1/2 cup mayonnaise | 1/2 cup shredded Parmesan cheese | 1/4 cup shredded mozzarella cheese | 2 cloves garlic, minced | Salt and pepper to taste

SERVINGS = Serves 6

MODE OF COOKING = Oven

PROCEDURE =

Preheat oven to 350°F (175°C).

In a bowl, mix together spinach, artichoke hearts, Greek yogurt, mayonnaise, Parmesan cheese, mozzarella cheese, garlic, salt, and pepper.

Transfer mixture to a baking dish and bake for 20-25 minutes, until hot and bubbly.

Serve with whole grain crackers or vegetable sticks.

NUTRITIONAL VALUES = 200 calories | 8g protein | 15g fat | 10g carbohydrates | 3g fiber

Shrimp Cocktail [Fish]

PREPARATION TIME = 20 minutes

INGREDIENTS = 1 lb large shrimp, peeled and deveined | 1 lemon, sliced | 1 bay leaf | 1/2 cup ketchup | 2 tbsp horseradish | 1 tbsp Worcestershire sauce | 1 tsp hot sauce | Salt and pepper to taste

SERVINGS = Serves 4

MODE OF COOKING = Stovetop

PROCEDURE =

In a pot, bring water to a boil. Add lemon slices, bay leaf, salt, and pepper.

Add shrimp and cook for 2-3 minutes, until pink and cooked through. Drain and chill in the refrigerator.

In a bowl, mix together ketchup, horseradish, Worcestershire sauce, and hot sauce.

Serve chilled shrimp with cocktail sauce.

NUTRITIONAL VALUES = 150 calories | 25g protein | 2g fat | 8g carbohydrates | 1g fiber

Roasted Red Pepper Hummus [Vegetarian]

PREPARATION TIME = 10 minutes

INGREDIENTS = 1 can (15 oz) chickpeas, drained and rinsed | 1 roasted red pepper, chopped | 2 tbsp tahini | 2 tbsp lemon juice | 1 clove garlic, minced | 1/4 tsp ground cumin | 2 tbsp olive oil | Salt and pepper to taste

SERVINGS = Serves 6

MODE OF COOKING = Blender

PROCEDURE =

In a blender, combine chickpeas, roasted red pepper, tahini, lemon juice, garlic, cumin, olive oil, salt, and pepper.

Blend until smooth, adding water as needed to reach desired consistency.

Serve with whole grain pita bread or vegetable sticks.

NUTRITIONAL VALUES = 150 calories | 5g protein | 8g fat | 15g carbohydrates | 5g fiber

Caprese Skewers [Vegetarian]

PREPARATION TIME = 15 minutes

INGREDIENTS = 1 pint cherry tomatoes | 8 oz fresh mozzarella balls | 1/4 cup fresh basil leaves | 2 tbsp olive oil | 1 tbsp balsamic vinegar | Salt and pepper to taste

SERVINGS = Serves 8

MODE OF COOKING – No-cook

PROCEDURE =

Thread cherry tomatoes, mozzarella balls, and basil leaves onto skewers.

In a small bowl, whisk together olive oil, balsamic vinegar, salt, and pepper.

Drizzle skewers with balsamic dressing before serving.

NUTRITIONAL VALUES = 100 calories | 5g protein | 8g fat | 2g carbohydrates | 1g fiber

Guacamole [Vegetarian]

PREPARATION TIME = 10 minutes

INGREDIENTS = 2 ripe avocados, mashed | 1/4 red onion, diced | 1 tomato, diced | 1 jalapeño, seeded and minced | 1/4 cup fresh cilantro, chopped | 1 lime, juiced | Salt and pepper to taste

SERVINGS = Serves 4

MODE OF COOKING = No-cook

PROCEDURE =

In a bowl, combine mashed avocado, red onion, tomato, jalapeño, cilantro, lime juice, salt, and pepper.

Mix gently until well combined.

Serve with whole grain tortilla chips or vegetable sticks.

NUTRITIONAL VALUES = 200 calories | 3g protein | 18g fat | 10g carbohydrates | 7g fiber

Smoked Salmon and Cucumber Rolls [Fish]

PREPARATION TIME = 15 minutes

INGREDIENTS = 4 oz smoked salmon | 1 cucumber, thinly sliced lengthwise | 4 oz cream cheese, softened | 1 tbsp chopped fresh dill | 1 tbsp lemon juice

SERVINGS = Serves 4

MODE OF COOKING = No-cook

PROCEDURE =

In a bowl, mix cream cheese, dill, and lemon juice until well combined.

Spread a thin layer of the cream cheese mixture onto each cucumber slice.

Place a slice of smoked salmon on top of the cream cheese and roll up tightly.

NUTRITIONAL VALUES = 150 calories | 8g protein | 12g fat | 3g carbohydrates | 1g fiber

Baked Zucchini Chips [Vegetarian]

PREPARATION TIME – 30 minutes

INGREDIENTS = 2 zucchini, thinly sliced | 1 tbsp olive oil | 1/4 tsp garlic powder | 1/4 tsp salt

SERVINGS = Serves 4

MODE OF COOKING = Oven

PROCEDURE =

Preheat oven to 425°F (220°C).

In a bowl, toss zucchini slices with olive oil, garlic powder, and salt.

Arrange zucchini slices in a single layer on a baking sheet lined with parchment paper.

Bake for 20-25 minutes, until crisp and golden brown.

NUTRITIONAL VALUES = 50 calories | 1g protein | 3g fat | 5g carbohydrates | 1g fiber

Roasted Chickpeas [Vegetarian]

PREPARATION TIME = 30 minutes

INGREDIENTS = 1 can (15 oz) chickpeas, drained and rinsed | 1 tbsp olive oil | 1 tsp ground cumin | 1 tsp smoked paprika | 1/2 tsp garlic powder | 1/4 tsp salt

SERVINGS = Serves 4

MODE OF COOKING = Oven

PROCEDURE =

Preheat oven to 400°F (200°C).

Pat chickpeas dry with a paper towel.

In a bowl, toss chickpeas with olive oil, cumin, smoked paprika, garlic powder, and salt.

Spread chickpeas in a single layer on a baking sheet.

Bake for 20-25 minutes, until crisp and golden brown.

NUTRITIONAL VALUES = 150 calories | 6g protein | 5g fat | 20g carbohydrates | 6g fiber

Stuffed Cherry Tomatoes [Vegetarian]

PREPARATION TIME = 20 minutes

INGREDIENTS = 1 pint cherry tomatoes | 1/2 cup ricotta cheese | 1/4 cup chopped fresh basil | 1 clove garlic, minced | Salt and pepper to taste

SERVINGS = Serves 6

MODE OF COOKING = No-cook

PROCEDURE =

Cut the tops off the cherry tomatoes and scoop out the seeds.

In a bowl, mix ricotta cheese, basil, garlic, salt, and pepper.

Spoon the ricotta mixture into the cherry tomatoes.

Serve chilled.

NUTRITIONAL VALUES = 100 calories | 5g protein | 6g fat | 5g carbohydrates | 1g fiber

Turkey and Avocado Roll-Ups [Meat]

PREPARATION TIME = 10 minutes

INGREDIENTS = 4 slices turkey breast | 1 avocado, sliced | 1 red bell pepper, thinly sliced | 4 lettuce leaves

SERVINGS = Serves 4

MODE OF COOKING = No-cook

PROCEDURE =

Place a slice of turkey breast on a cutting board.

Layer avocado, bell pepper, and lettuce leaf on top.

Roll up tightly and secure with a toothpick if needed.

Repeat with remaining ingredients.

NUTRITIONAL VALUES = 150 calories | 10g protein | 10g fat | 5g carbohydrates | 3g fiber

Quick and Easy Recipes (Under 15 Minutes):

Greek Yogurt Ranch Dip [Vegetarian]

PREPARATION TIME = 5 minutes

INGREDIENTS = 1 cup Greek yogurt | 1 tbsp ranch seasoning mix | 1/4 tsp garlic powder | 1/4 tsp onion powder | Salt and pepper to taste

SERVINGS = Serves 4

MODE OF COOKING = No-cook

PROCEDURE =

In a bowl, mix Greek yogurt, ranch seasoning mix, garlic powder, onion powder, salt, and pepper.

Serve with vegetable sticks.

NUTRITIONAL VALUES = 50 calories | 5g protein | 1g fat | 5g carbohydrates | 0g fiber

Watermelon and Feta Skewers [Vegetarian]

PREPARATION TIME = 10 minutes

INGREDIENTS = 2 cups watermelon, cubed | 1/2 cup feta cheese, cubed | 1/4 cup fresh mint leaves

SERVINGS = Serves 6

MODE OF COOKING = No-cook

PROCEDURE =

Thread watermelon cubes, feta cubes, and mint leaves onto skewers.

Serve chilled.

NUTRITIONAL VALUES = 50 calories | 2g protein | 3g fat | 5g carbohydrates | 0g fiber

Peanut Butter and Banana Bites [Vegetarian]

PREPARATION TIME = 10 minutes

INGREDIENTS = 2 bananas, sliced | 1/4 cup peanut butter | 1/4 cup granola

SERVINGS = Serves 4

MODE OF COOKING = No-cook

PROCEDURE =

Spread a small amount of peanut butter onto each banana slice.

Top with granola.

Serve immediately.

NUTRITIONAL VALUES = 150 calories | 4g protein | 8g fat | 20g carbohydrates | 3g fiber

Cucumber and Hummus Bites [Vegetarian]

PREPARATION TIME = 10 minutes

INGREDIENTS = 1 cucumber, sliced | 1/2 cup hummus | 1/4 tsp smoked paprika

SERVINGS = Serves 4

MODE OF COOKING = No-cook

PROCEDURE =

Spread a small amount of hummus onto each cucumber slice.

Sprinkle with smoked paprika.

Serve chilled.

NUTRITIONAL VALUES = 100 calories | 4g protein | 6g fat | 10g carbohydrates | 3g fiber

Caprese Salad Skewers [Vegetarian]

PREPARATION TIME = 10 minutes

INGREDIENTS – 1 cup cherry tomatoes | 1 cup fresh mozzarella balls | 1/4 cup fresh basil leaves | 2 tbsp balsamic vinegar | Salt and pepper to taste

SERVINGS = Serves 6

MODE OF COOKING = No-cook

PROCEDURE =

Thread cherry tomatoes, mozzarella balls, and basil leaves onto skewers.

Drizzle with balsamic vinegar and season with salt and pepper.

Serve immediately.

NUTRITIONAL VALUES = 100 calories | 5g protein | 6g fat | 5g carbohydrates | 1g fiber

Chapter 13: Desserts and Treats

Baked Cinnamon Apples [Vegetarian]

PREPARATION TIME = 40 minutes

INGREDIENTS = 4 apples, cored and sliced | 1 tbsp coconut oil, melted | 1 tsp ground cinnamon | 1/4 tsp ground nutmeg | 1 tbsp maple syrup

SERVINGS = Serves 4

MODE OF COOKING = Oven

PROCEDURE =

Preheat oven to 375°F (190°C).

In a bowl, toss apple slices with melted coconut oil, cinnamon, nutmeg, and maple syrup.

Arrange apple slices in a baking dish and bake for 25-30 minutes, until tender.

NUTRITIONAL VALUES = 100 calories | 1g protein | 3g fat | 20g carbohydrates | 4g fiber

Honey-Glazed Grilled Peaches

PREPARATION TIME = 15 minutes

INGREDIENTS = 4 ripe peaches, halved and pitted | 2 tbsp honey | 1 tbsp olive oil | 1/4 tsp ground cinnamon

SERVINGS = Serves 4

MODE OF COOKING = Grill

PROCEDURE =

Preheat grill to medium-high heat.

In a small bowl, whisk together honey, olive oil, and cinnamon.

Brush peach halves with the honey mixture.

Grill peaches, cut side down, for 4-5 minutes until lightly charred and tender.

NUTRITIONAL VALUES = 100 calories | 1g protein | 3g fat | 20g carbohydrates | 2g fiber

Greek Yogurt Berry Parfaits

PREPARATION TIME = 10 minutes

INGREDIENTS = 2 cups Greek yogurt | 1 cup mixed berries (strawberries, raspberries, blueberries) | 1/4 cup chopped walnuts | 2 tbsp honey

SERVINGS = Serves 4

MODE OF COOKING = No-cook

PROCEDURE =

In parfait glasses or small jars, layer 1/4 cup Greek yogurt, followed by 2 tbsp berries and 1/2 tbsp walnuts.

Repeat layers once more.

Drizzle each parfait with 1/2 tbsp honey.

NUTRITIONAL VALUES = 200 calories | 10g protein | 10g fat | 20g carbohydrates | 2g fiber

Almond Butter Stuffed Dates

PREPARATION TIME = 10 minutes

INGREDIENTS = 12 Medjool dates, pitted | 1/4 cup almond butter | 1/4 cup shredded unsweetened coconut

SERVINGS = Serves 6

MODE OF COOKING = No-cook

PROCEDURE =

Slice dates lengthwise, being careful not to cut all the way through.

Spoon about 1 tsp almond butter into each date.

Sprinkle stuffed dates with shredded coconut.

NUTRITIONAL VALUES = 150 calories | 3g protein | 7g fat | 20g carbohydrates | 4g fiber

Cinnamon-Spiced Baked Apples

PREPARATION TIME = 40 minutes

INGREDIENTS = 4 large apples, cored | 1/4 cup raisins | 1/4 cup chopped pecans | 2 tbsp honey | 1 tsp ground cinnamon | 1/4 tsp ground nutmeg

SERVINGS = Serves 4

MODE OF COOKING = Oven

PROCEDURE =

Preheat oven to 375°F (190°C).

In a small bowl, mix raisins, pecans, honey, cinnamon, and nutmeg.

Stuff each apple core with the raisin mixture.

Place apples in a baking dish and bake for 30-35 minutes, until tender.

NUTRITIONAL VALUES = 200 calories | 2g protein | 8g fat | 35g carbohydrates | 6g fiber

Peach Crisp [Vegetarian]

PREPARATION TIME = 40 minutes

INGREDIENTS = 4 cups sliced peaches | 1 cup rolled oats | 1/2 cup almond flour | 1/4 cup coconut oil, melted | 1/4 cup maple syrup | 1 tsp ground cinnamon | 1/4 tsp salt

SERVINGS = Serves 6

MODE OF COOKING = Oven

PROCEDURE =

Preheat oven to 375°F (190°C).

In a bowl, toss peach slices with 2 tbsp maple syrup.

In another bowl, mix oats, almond flour, coconut oil, remaining maple syrup, cinnamon, and salt until crumbly.

Place peaches in a baking dish and sprinkle oat mixture on top.

Bake for 30-35 minutes, until peaches are tender and topping is golden brown.

NUTRITIONAL VALUES = 300 calories | 5g protein | 15g fat | 40g carbohydrates | 5g fiber

Pumpkin Spice Energy Bites [Vegetarian]

PREPARATION TIME = 15 minutes

INGREDIENTS = 1 cup pitted dates | 1/2 cup pumpkin puree | 1/2 cup rolled oats | 1/4 cup almond butter | 1 tsp pumpkin pie spice | 1/4 tsp salt

SERVINGS = Makes 12 bites

MODE OF COOKING = No-cook

PROCEDURE =

In a food processor, combine dates, pumpkin puree, oats, almond butter, pumpkin pie spice, and salt.

Pulse until mixture comes together and forms a dough.

Roll dough into 12 balls.

Store in the refrigerator.

NUTRITIONAL VALUES (per bite): 100 calories | 2g protein | 3g fat | 20g carbohydrates | 3g fiber

Raspberry Chia Jam Bars [Vegetarian]

PREPARATION TIME = 30 minutes

INGREDIENTS = 1 cup raspberries | 2 tbsp chia seeds | 2 tbsp maple syrup | 1 cup almond flour | 1/2 cup rolled oats | 1/4 cup coconut oil, melted | 1/4 tsp salt

SERVINGS = Makes 8 bars

MODE OF COOKING = Oven

PROCEDURE =

Preheat oven to 350°F (175°C).

In a saucepan, cook raspberries, chia seeds, and maple syrup over medium heat until thickened, about 5 minutes.

In a bowl, mix almond flour, oats, coconut oil, and salt until crumbly.

Press 2/3 of the oat mixture into a lined 8x8 inch baking pan.

Spread raspberry chia jam over the crust.

Sprinkle remaining oat mixture on top.

Bake for 20-25 minutes, until golden brown.

Let cool completely before cutting into bars.

NUTRITIONAL VALUES (per bar): 200 calories | 5g protein | 15g fat | 15g carbohydrates | 5g fiber

Strawberry Banana Nice Cream [Vegetarian]

PREPARATION TIME = 5 minutes

INGREDIENTS = 2 frozen bananas | 1 cup frozen strawberries | 1/4 cup almond milk | 1 tsp vanilla extract

SERVINGS = Serves 2

MODE OF COOKING = Blender

PROCEDURE =

In a blender, combine frozen bananas, frozen strawberries, almond milk, and vanilla extract.

Blend until smooth and creamy, scraping down the sides as needed.

Serve immediately.

NUTRITIONAL VALUES = 150 calories | 2g protein | 2g fat | 35g carbohydrates | 6g fiber

Tropical Fruit Salad [Vegetarian]

PREPARATION TIME = 15 minutes

INGREDIENTS = 1 mango, diced | 1 papaya, diced | 1 cup pineapple chunks | 1 cup kiwi slices | 1/4 cup fresh mint leaves, chopped | 1 lime, juiced

SERVINGS = Serves 4

MODE OF COOKING = No-cook

PROCEDURE =

In a large bowl, combine mango, papaya, pineapple, kiwi, and mint leaves.

Drizzle with lime juice and toss gently to combine.

Serve chilled.

NUTRITIONAL VALUES = 100 calories | 1g protein | 0g fat | 25g carbohydrates | 4g fiber

Quick and Easy Recipes (Under 15 Minutes):

Banana Almond Butter Ice Cream [Vegetarian]

PREPARATION TIME = 5 minutes

INGREDIENTS = 2 frozen bananas | 2 tbsp almond butter | 1/4 tsp ground cinnamon

SERVINGS = Serves 2

MODE OF COOKING = Blender

PROCEDURE =

In a blender, combine frozen bananas, almond butter, and cinnamon.

Blend until smooth and creamy, scraping down the sides as needed.

Serve immediately.

NUTRITIONAL VALUES = 200 calories | 4g protein | 10g fat | 25g carbohydrates | 4g fiber

Honey-Cinnamon Ricotta Dip with Fruit

PREPARATION TIME = 5 minutes

INGREDIENTS = 1 cup ricotta cheese | 2 tbsp honey | 1/2 tsp ground cinnamon | 2 cups mixed fruit (apples, pears, grapes), sliced

SERVINGS = Serves 4

MODE OF COOKING = No-cook

PROCEDURE =

In a bowl, mix ricotta cheese, honey, and cinnamon until well combined.

Serve the dip alongside sliced fruit for dipping.

NUTRITIONAL VALUES = 200 calories | 8g protein | 8g fat | 25g carbohydrates | 3g fiber

Greek Yogurt Bark [Vegetarian]

PREPARATION TIME = 5 minutes (plus 2 hours freezing time)

INGREDIENTS = 2 cups Greek yogurt | 1/4 cup honey | 1 tsp vanilla extract | 1/2 cup mixed berries

SERVINGS = Serves 6

MODE OF COOKING = Freezer

PROCEDURE =

In a bowl, mix Greek yogurt, honey, and vanilla extract.

Spread mixture onto a parchment-lined baking sheet.

Sprinkle mixed berries on top.

Freeze for at least 2 hours, then break into pieces.

NUTRITIONAL VALUES = 100 calories | 5g protein | 2g fat | 15g carbohydrates | 1g fiber

Yogurt-Dipped Frozen Berries

PREPARATION TIME = 10 minutes (plus 2 hours freezing time)

INGREDIENTS = 2 cups mixed berries (strawberries, raspberries, blueberries) | 1 cup Greek yogurt | 1 tbsp honey

SERVINGS = Serves 4

MODE OF COOKING = Freezer

PROCEDURE =

Line a baking sheet with parchment paper.

In a bowl, mix Greek yogurt and honey until well combined.

Dip each berry into the yogurt mixture, coating evenly, and place on the prepared baking sheet.

Freeze for at least 2 hours, until solid.

NUTRITIONAL VALUES = 100 calories | 5g protein | 2g fat | 15g carbohydrates | 3g fiber

Chocolate-Drizzled Fruit Skewers

PREPARATION TIME = 15 minutes

INGREDIENTS = 2 cups mixed fruit (pineapple, mango, kiwi), cubed | 1/4 cup dark chocolate (70% cacao), melted

SERVINGS = Serves 4

MODE OF COOKING = No-cook

PROCEDURE =

Thread fruit cubes onto skewers.

Drizzle melted dark chocolate over the fruit skewers.

Refrigerate for 5-10 minutes, until the chocolate has set.

NUTRITIONAL VALUES = 150 calories | 2g protein | 5g fat | 25g carbohydrates | 4g fiber

Chapter 14: Beverages and Smoothies

Carrot and Orange Juice [Vegetarian]

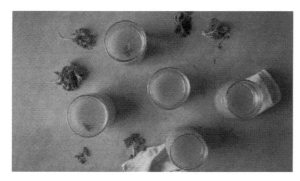

PREPARATION TIME = 10 minutes

INGREDIENTS = 4 carrots | 2 oranges, peeled

SERVINGS = 2 servings

MODE OF COOKING = Juicer

PROCEDURE =

Wash and chop carrots and oranges to fit your juicer.

Feed ingredients through the juicer and collect the juice.

Stir and serve immediately.

NUTRITIONAL VALUES = 100 calories | 2g protein | 0g fat | 25g carbohydrates | 5g fiber

Spinach and Apple Smoothie [Vegetarian]

PREPARATION TIME = 5 minutes

INGREDIENTS = 2 cups spinach | 1 green apple, cubed | 1 cup almond milk | 1/2 cup ice cubes

SERVINGS = 1 serving

MODE OF COOKING = Blender

PROCEDURE =

In a blender, combine spinach, apple, almond milk, and ice cubes.

Blend until smooth.

NUTRITIONAL VALUES = 150 calories | 5g protein | 3g fat | 30g carbohydrates | 8g fiber

Blueberry and Avocado Smoothie

PREPARATION TIME = 5 minutes

INGREDIENTS = 1 cup blueberries | 1/2 ripe avocado | 1 cup coconut milk | 1/2 cup ice cubes

SERVINGS = 1 serving

MODE OF COOKING = Blender

PROCEDURE =

In a blender, combine blueberries, avocado, coconut milk, and ice cubes.

Blend until smooth.

NUTRITIONAL VALUES = 300 calories | 4g protein | 20g fat | 30g carbohydrates | 8g fiber

Ginger Lemonade [Gluten-Free]

PREPARATION TIME = 10 minutes

INGREDIENTS = 4 lemons, juiced | 1 piece of ginger (1 inch), grated | 4 cups water | 2 tablespoons honey

SERVINGS = 4 servings

MODE OF COOKING = No-cook

PROCEDURE =

In a pitcher, combine lemon juice, grated ginger, water, and honey.

Stir well until honey is dissolved.

Serve over ice.

NUTRITIONAL VALUES = 50 calories | 0g protein | 0g fat | 15g carbohydrates | 0g fiber

Strawberry and Greek Yogurt Smoothie

PREPARATION TIME = 5 minutes

INGREDIENTS = 1 cup strawberries | 1/2 cup Greek yogurt | 1/2 cup milk | 1 tablespoon honey | 1/2 cup ice cubes

SERVINGS = 1 serving

MODE OF COOKING = Blender

PROCEDURE =

In a blender, combine strawberries, Greek yogurt, milk, honey, and ice cubes.

Blend until smooth.

NUTRITIONAL VALUES = 200 calories | 10g protein | 3g fat | 35g carbohydrates | 4g fiber

Coffee and Almond Milk Frappé

PREPARATION TIME = 5 minutes

INGREDIENTS = 1 cup cold brewed coffee | 1/2 cup almond milk | 1 tablespoon maple syrup | 1 cup ice cubes

SERVINGS = 1 serving

MODE OF COOKING = Blender

PROCEDURE =

In a blender, combine cold brewed coffee, almond milk, maple syrup, and ice cubes.

Blend until smooth.

NUTRITIONAL VALUES = 100 calories | 1g protein | 3g fat | 20g carbohydrates | 1g fiber

Green Tea with Lime and Mint [Gluten-Free]

PREPARATION TIME = 5 minutes

INGREDIENTS = 2 green tea bags | 2 cups hot water | 1 lime, juiced | 2 sprigs fresh mint

SERVINGS = 2 servings

MODE OF COOKING = No-cook

PROCEDURE =

Steep green tea bags in hot water for 3-5 minutes. Remove bags.

Stir in lime juice.

Serve with fresh mint sprigs.

NUTRITIONAL VALUES = 0 calories | 0g protein | 0g fat | 5g carbohydrates | 0g fiber

Papaya and Mango Smoothie

PREPARATION TIME = 5 minutes

INGREDIENTS = 1 cup papaya, cubed | 1 cup mango, cubed | 1 cup coconut milk | 1/2 cup ice cubes

SERVINGS = 1 serving

MODE OF COOKING = Blender

PROCEDURE =

In a blender, combine papaya, mango, coconut milk, and ice cubes.

Blend until smooth.

NUTRITIONAL VALUES = 300 calories | 3g protein | 20g fat | 35g carbohydrates | 5g fiber

Quick and Easy Mixed Recipes (Under 5 Minutes):

Melon and Prosciutto Skewers [Quick]

PREPARATION TIME = 5 minutes

INGREDIENTS = 1 cup cantaloupe, cubed | 1 cup honeydew, cubed | 4 slices prosciutto, cut into strips | 8 small skewers

SERVINGS = 4 servings

MODE OF COOKING = No-cook

PROCEDURE =

Thread cantaloupe, honeydew, and prosciutto strips onto skewers, alternating ingredients.

NUTRITIONAL VALUES = 50 calories | 5g protein | 1g fat | 5g carbohydrates | 1g fiber

Watermelon Feta Bites [Vegetarian]

PREPARATION TIME = 5 minutes

INGREDIENTS = 2 cups watermelon, cubed | 1/2 cup feta cheese, cubed | 1/4 cup fresh mint leaves | 1 tablespoon olive oil | 1 tablespoon balsamic vinegar

SERVINGS = 4 servings

MODE OF COOKING = No-cook

PROCEDURE =

In a bowl, combine watermelon, feta cheese, and mint leaves.

Drizzle with olive oil and balsamic vinegar.

Toss gently to coat.

NUTRITIONAL VALUES = 100 calories | 3g protein | 6g fat | 10g carbohydrates | 1g fiber

Chapter 15: DIY Staples and Condiments

Hummus [Vegetarian]

PREPARATION TIME = 10 minutes

INGREDIENTS = 1 can (15 oz) chickpeas, drained and rinsed | 1/4 cup tahini | 1/4 cup lemon juice | 2 cloves garlic | 1/4 tsp ground cumin | 2 tbsp olive oil | Salt to taste

SERVINGS = Yields about 1 1/2 cups

MODE OF COOKING = Food Processor

PROCEDURE =

In a food processor, combine chickpeas, tahini, lemon juice, garlic, cumin, and salt.

While the food processor is running, gradually add olive oil until the desired consistency is reached.

If the hummus is too thick, add 1-2 tbsp of water or aquafaba (chickpea cooking liquid).

Taste and adjust seasoning as needed.

Store hummus in an airtight container in the refrigerator for up to 1 week.

NUTRITIONAL VALUES (per 2 tbsp): 100 calories | 3g protein | 7g fat | 7g carbohydrates | 2g fiber

Chicken Bone Broth

PREPARATION TIME = 10 minutes (plus 12-24 hours simmering time)

INGREDIENTS = 2-3 lbs chicken bones | 1 onion, quartered | 2 carrots, chopped | 2 celery stalks, chopped | 2 tbsp apple cider vinegar | 1 bay leaf | 1 tsp peppercorns | Water to cover

SERVINGS = Yields about 8-10 cups

MODE OF COOKING = Stovetop or Slow Cooker

PROCEDURE =

Place chicken bones, onion, carrots, celery, apple cider vinegar, bay leaf, and peppercorns in a large pot or slow cooker.

Cover with water, leaving about 2 inches of space at the top.

If using a pot, bring the mixture to a boil, then reduce heat and simmer for 12-24 hours. If using a slow cooker, cook on low for 12-24 hours.

Strain the broth through a fine-mesh sieve and discard the solids.

Let the broth cool, then store in airtight containers in the refrigerator for up to 1 week, or freeze for up to 3 months.

NUTRITIONAL VALUES (per 1 cup): 50 calories | 5g protein | 2g fat | 0g carbohydrates | 0g fiber

Almond Butter [Vegetarian]

PREPARATION TIME = 15 minutes

INGREDIENTS = 2 cups raw almonds | 1-2 tbsp coconut oil (optional)

SERVINGS = Yields about 1 cup

MODE OF COOKING = Food Processor

PROCEDURE =

Preheat oven to 350°F (175°C).

Spread almonds on a baking sheet and toast for 8-10 minutes, stirring occasionally, until lightly golden and fragrant.

Let almonds cool for a few minutes.

In a food processor, process toasted almonds for 5-10 minutes, scraping down the sides as needed, until a smooth butter forms.

If desired, add coconut oil to help achieve a smoother consistency.

Store almond butter in an airtight container in the refrigerator for up to 2 months.

NUTRITIONAL VALUES (per 2 tbsp): 200 calories | 7g protein | 18g fat | 6g carbohydrates | 4g fiber

Ghee

PREPARATION TIME = 20 minutes

INGREDIENTS = 1 lb unsalted butter

SERVINGS = Yields about 1 1/2 cups

MODE OF COOKING = Stovetop

PROCEDURE =

Cut butter into cubes and place in a saucepan over medium heat.

Let the butter melt and bring to a simmer. Reduce heat to low and continue to simmer, stirring occasionally, until the milk solids separate and sink to the bottom, and the butter becomes clear, about 15-20 minutes.

Strain the ghee through a cheesecloth or coffee filter into a clean, dry jar.

Store ghee in an airtight container at room temperature for up to 1 month, or in the refrigerator for up to 3 months.

NUTRITIONAL VALUES (per 1 tbsp): 120 calories | 0g protein | 14g fat | 0g carbohydrates | 0g fiber

Cashew Cheese [Vegetarian]

PREPARATION TIME = 10 minutes (plus soaking time)

INGREDIENTS = 1 cup raw cashews | 1/4 cup water | 2 tbsp lemon juice | 1 tbsp nutritional yeast | 1/2 tsp garlic powder | 1/2 tsp salt

SERVINGS = Yields about 1 cup

MODE OF COOKING = Blender

PROCEDURE =

Soak cashews in water for at least 2 hours or overnight. Drain and rinse.

In a blender, combine soaked cashews, water, lemon juice, nutritional yeast, garlic powder, and salt.

Blend on high speed for 2-3 minutes, until smooth and creamy, scraping down the sides as needed.

Use as a dairy-free alternative to cheese in recipes or as a spread.

Store cashew cheese in the refrigerator for up to 5 days.

NUTRITIONAL VALUES (per 2 tbsp): 100 calories | 3g protein | 8g fat | 5g carbohydrates | 1g fiber

Dijon Mustard

PREPARATION TIME = 10 minutes (plus 24-48 hours resting time)

INGREDIENTS = 1/2 cup yellow mustard seeds | 1/4 cup brown mustard seeds | 1/2 cup white wine vinegar | 1/2 cup water | 1 tsp salt | 1 tbsp honey (optional)

SERVINGS = Yields about 1 1/2 cups

MODE OF COOKING = No-cook

PROCEDURE =

In a bowl, combine yellow mustard seeds, brown mustard seeds, white wine vinegar, water, and salt. Cover and let sit at room temperature for 24-48 hours.

Transfer the mixture to a blender and blend until the desired consistency is reached, adding more water if needed.

If desired, add honey and blend to combine.

Store Dijon mustard in an airtight container in the refrigerator for up to 1 month.

NUTRITIONAL VALUES (per 1 tbsp): 20 calories | 1g protein | 1g fat | 2g carbohydrates | 1g fiber

Sriracha Sauce

PREPARATION TIME = 20 minutes

INGREDIENTS = 1 lb red jalapeño peppers, stemmed and chopped | 6 cloves garlic, peeled | 1/4 cup white vinegar | 1 tbsp sugar | 1 tsp salt

SERVINGS = Yields about 1 1/2 cups

MODE OF COOKING = Stovetop

PROCEDURE =

In a saucepan, combine jalapeño peppers, garlic, white vinegar, sugar, and salt.

Bring the mixture to a boil, then reduce heat and simmer for 10-15 minutes, until the peppers are soft.

Transfer the mixture to a blender and blend until smooth.

Strain the sauce through a fine-mesh sieve to remove any seeds or skin.

Store sriracha sauce in an airtight container in the refrigerator for up to 1 month.

NUTRITIONAL VALUES (per 1 tbsp): 10 calories | 0g protein | 0g fat | 2g carbohydrates | 0g fiber

Tomato Sauce [Vegetarian]

PREPARATION TIME = 30 minutes

INGREDIENTS = 2 tbsp olive oil | 1 onion, diced | 4 cloves garlic, minced | 2 cans (28 oz each)

whole peeled tomatoes | 1 tsp dried basil | 1 tsp dried oregano | Salt and pepper to taste

SERVINGS = Yields about 6 cups

MODE OF COOKING = Stovetop

PROCEDURE =

In a large pot, heat olive oil over medium heat. Add onion and garlic, and cook until softened, about 5 minutes.

Add tomatoes (with their juice), basil, oregano, salt, and pepper. Break up the tomatoes with a spoon.

Bring the mixture to a boil, then reduce heat and simmer for 20-25 minutes, stirring occasionally, until thickened.

Use an immersion blender to puree the sauce until smooth, or leave it chunky if desired.

Taste and adjust seasoning as needed.

Store tomato sauce in an airtight container in the refrigerator for up to 1 week, or freeze for up to 3 months.

NUTRITIONAL VALUES (per 1/2 cup): 50 calories | 1g protein | 3g fat | 5g carbohydrates | 1g fiber

Quick and Easy Mixed Recipes (Under 5 Minutes):

Gluten-Free Taco Seasoning [Quick]

PREPARATION TIME = 5 minutes

INGREDIENTS = 1 tbsp chili powder | 1 tsp ground cumin | 1 tsp smoked paprika | 1 tsp garlic powder | 1 tsp onion powder | 1 tsp dried oregano | 1/2 tsp salt

SERVINGS = Yields about 3 tbsp

MODE OF COOKING = No-cook

PROCEDURE =

In a small bowl, combine chili powder, ground cumin, smoked paprika, garlic powder, onion powder, dried oregano, and salt.

Mix well to combine.

Store taco seasoning in an airtight container at room temperature for up to 6 months.

NUTRITIONAL VALUES (per 1 tsp): 5 calories | 0g protein | 0g fat | 1g carbohydrates | 0g fiber

Almond Flour [Vegetarian, Gluten-Free]

PREPARATION TIME = 5 minutes

INGREDIENTS = 1 cup raw almonds

SERVINGS = Yields about 1 cup

MODE OF COOKING = Food Processor

PROCEDURE =

In a food processor, process almonds for 30-60 seconds, until they reach a fine, flour-like consistency.

Be careful not to over-process, as this may cause the almonds to turn into almond butter.

Store almond flour in an airtight container in the refrigerator for up to 1 month, or in the freezer for up to 3 months.

NUTRITIONAL VALUES (per 1/4 cup): 160 calories | 6g protein | 14g fat | 6g carbohydrates | 3g fiber.

Part V: Living Well with Arthritis

Chapter 16: Other Lifestyle Factors for Managing Arthritis

16.1 The importance of regular exercise

While adopting an anti-inflammatory diet is a crucial step in managing arthritis, regular exercise is equally vital for maintaining joint health and reducing pain. Many people with arthritis hesitate to exercise, fearing that it will exacerbate their symptoms. However, the right kind of physical activity can actually help alleviate pain, improve mobility, and enhance overall well-being.

The Benefits of Exercise for Arthritis

Engaging in regular exercise offers numerous benefits for individuals with arthritis. First and foremost, it helps maintain joint flexibility and range of motion. When you have arthritis, your joints can become stiff and painful, making it difficult to perform everyday tasks. By exercising regularly, you keep your joints moving and lubricated, reducing stiffness and promoting flexibility.

Moreover, exercise strengthens the muscles surrounding your joints, providing them with greater support and stability. Strong muscles help absorb the shock and pressure placed on your joints during movement, ultimately reducing pain and inflammation. This is particularly important for weight-bearing joints like the knees, hips, and ankles, which are commonly affected by arthritis.

In addition to its physical benefits, exercise also has a positive impact on mental health. Living with chronic pain can lead to feelings of depression, anxiety, and frustration. Regular physical activity releases endorphins, the body's natural mood-boosters, which can help combat these negative emotions and improve overall well-being.

Choosing the Right Exercises

When it comes to exercising with arthritis, it's essential to choose activities that are gentle on your joints while still providing the necessary benefits. Low-impact exercises are ideal, as they put minimal stress on your joints and reduce the risk of injury. Some excellent options include:

Swimming and water aerobics: The buoyancy of water supports your body weight, reducing the impact on your joints while providing gentle resistance to build strength.

Walking: This simple yet effective exercise is easy on the joints and can be done almost anywhere. Start with short walks and gradually increase the duration and intensity as your fitness improves.

Cycling: Whether on a stationary bike or outdoors, cycling is a low-impact activity that strengthens the muscles around your knees without putting undue stress on the joints.

Yoga and Tai Chi: These gentle, flowing exercises promote flexibility, balance, and relaxation. Many poses can be modified to accommodate your individual needs and limitations.

Strength training: Using light weights or resistance bands, strength training helps build muscle and support your joints. Focus on exercises that target the muscles surrounding your affected joints.

Before starting any exercise program, it's crucial to consult with your healthcare provider or a physical therapist who specializes in arthritis. They can help you develop a personalized exercise plan that takes into account your specific needs, limitations, and goals.

Staying Motivated and Consistent

Incorporating regular exercise into your lifestyle can be challenging, especially when you're dealing with the pain and fatigue of arthritis. However, staying motivated and consistent is key to reaping the long-term benefits. Here are some tips to help you stay on track:

- Start small: Begin with short, manageable exercise sessions and gradually increase the duration and intensity as your fitness improves.
- Set realistic goals: Focus on achievable milestones, such as walking for 10 minutes a day or attending a yoga class once a week. Celebrate your progress along the way.
- Find an exercise buddy: Having a friend or family member to exercise with can provide motivation, accountability, and support.
- Mix it up: Vary your exercise routine to prevent boredom and challenge different muscle groups. Try new activities that you enjoy and look forward to.
- Listen to your body: Pay attention to your body's signals and adjust your exercise accordingly. If you experience increased pain or fatigue, take a break or try a gentler activity.
- Remember, the key to success is consistency. Even small amounts of regular exercise can make a significant difference in managing your arthritis symptoms and improving your overall quality of life.

By combining an anti-inflammatory diet with a regular exercise routine, you'll be well on your way to living a healthier, more active life with arthritis. Don't let joint pain hold you back from enjoying the activities you love. With the right tools and mindset, you can take control of your arthritis and thrive. Scan the QR code to access our Arthritis-Friendly Exercise Guide, a comprehensive resource featuring exercises designed to complement your anti-inflammatory diet and amplify your results. This guide will help you safely and effectively incorporate physical activity into your daily life, empowering you to manage your arthritis symptoms and reclaim your vitality.

16.2 Stress management techniques

Living with arthritis can be incredibly stressful, both physically and emotionally. Chronic pain, fatigue, and the limitations imposed by the condition can take a toll on your mental well-being, leading to feelings of anxiety, depression, and helplessness. However, effectively managing stress is a crucial component of a comprehensive arthritis management plan, as high stress levels can exacerbate inflammation and worsen symptoms.

The Mind-Body Connection

The link between stress and arthritis is complex and multifaceted. When you experience stress, your body releases hormones like cortisol and adrenaline, which trigger the "fight or flight" response. While this response is beneficial in short-term, acute stress situations, chronic stress can lead to persistently elevated levels of these hormones, contributing to systemic inflammation.

Moreover, stress can cause muscle tension, which can further aggravate joint pain and stiffness. This, in turn, can lead to a vicious cycle of pain, stress, and more pain. By learning to manage stress effectively, you can break this cycle and create a more positive, supportive environment for your body to heal.

Effective Stress Management Techniques

There are numerous stress management techniques that can help you cope with the challenges of living with arthritis. Some of the most effective strategies include:

- Mindfulness meditation: This practice involves focusing your attention on the present moment, observing your thoughts and feelings without judgment. Regular mindfulness meditation has been shown to reduce stress, anxiety, and depression, as well as improve pain management.
- Deep breathing exercises: Controlled, deep breathing can help activate the body's relaxation response, reducing muscle tension and promoting a sense of calm. Try taking slow, deep breaths from your diaphragm, counting to four as you inhale and exhale.
- Progressive muscle relaxation: This technique involves systematically tensing and relaxing different muscle groups throughout your body, helping you identify and release areas of tension. Start with your toes and work your way up to your head, holding each contraction for a few seconds before releasing.
- Guided imagery: Using your imagination to visualize peaceful, calming scenes can help reduce stress and promote relaxation. Close your eyes and picture yourself in a tranquil setting, engaging all your senses to make the experience as vivid as possible.
- Journaling: Writing about your thoughts, feelings, and experiences can be a cathartic way to process stress and gain a new perspective on your challenges. Set aside a few minutes each day to jot down your reflections, focusing on gratitude and positive aspects of your life.

- Hobbies and creative pursuits: Engaging in activities that bring you joy and fulfillment can be a powerful stress-buster. Whether it's painting, gardening, or playing a musical instrument, make time for hobbies that allow you to express yourself and find a sense of purpose.
- Social support: Connecting with others who understand your experiences can provide a invaluable source of emotional support and practical advice. Join a local arthritis support group, participate in online forums, or confide in trusted friends and family members.

Incorporating Stress Management into Your Daily Life

To reap the full benefits of stress management, it's essential to make these practices a consistent part of your daily routine. Set aside dedicated time each day for relaxation and self-care, even if it's just a few minutes. Consider starting your day with a brief meditation or deep breathing session, and wind down in the evening with a relaxing hobby or journaling.

Remember, stress management is a skill that requires practice and patience. Be kind to yourself as you explore different techniques and find what works best for you. If you find yourself struggling to cope with stress despite your best efforts, don't hesitate to seek professional help from a therapist or counselor who specializes in chronic pain management.

By prioritizing stress management alongside your anti-inflammatory diet and exercise routine, you'll be better equipped to navigate the challenges of living with arthritis. Reduced stress levels can lead to improved pain management, increased energy, and a greater sense of overall well-being, allowing you to focus on the things that truly matter in your life.

16.3 Adequate rest and sleep

During sleep, your body undergoes important restorative processes that help repair damaged tissues, reduce inflammation, and regulate pain signals. When you don't get enough quality sleep, these processes are disrupted, leading to increased pain sensitivity, fatigue, and emotional distress.

Moreover, poor sleep can contribute to a weakened immune system, making you more susceptible to illnesses and flare-ups. Adequate sleep, on the other hand, helps bolster your body's natural defenses, allowing you to better manage your arthritis symptoms and maintain overall health.

Tips for Improving Sleep Quality

If you're struggling with sleep disturbances related to your arthritis, there are several strategies you can employ to improve your sleep quality and ensure you're getting the rest you need:

- Stick to a consistent sleep schedule: Go to bed and wake up at the same time every day, even on weekends. This helps regulate your body's internal clock and establish a healthy sleep-wake cycle.

- Create a relaxing bedtime routine: Develop a soothing pre-sleep ritual that helps you unwind and prepare for rest. This might include taking a warm bath, reading a book, or practicing gentle stretches or relaxation techniques.

- Optimize your sleep environment: Ensure your bedroom is cool, dark, and quiet. Invest in a comfortable, supportive mattress and pillows that minimize pressure on your joints.

- Manage pain proactively: Take steps to alleviate pain and discomfort before bed, such as applying heat or cold therapy, using topical pain relievers, or practicing relaxation techniques like deep breathing or progressive muscle relaxation.

- Avoid stimulants and large meals close to bedtime: Caffeine, alcohol, and nicotine can interfere with sleep quality, so it's best to avoid these substances in the hours leading up to bedtime. Similarly, eating a heavy meal close to sleep can cause discomfort and disrupt rest.

- Exercise regularly: Engaging in regular physical activity can help improve sleep quality and duration. Aim for low-impact exercises like swimming, cycling, or yoga, and avoid vigorous exercise close to bedtime.

- Manage stress and anxiety: Stress and anxiety can significantly impact sleep quality. Practice stress management techniques like mindfulness meditation, journaling, or deep breathing exercises to help calm your mind and promote relaxation.

The Role of Rest in Arthritis Management

In addition to getting enough sleep at night, it's important to incorporate periods of rest throughout your day. When you have arthritis, it's essential to listen to your body and give it the breaks it needs to recharge and recover.

This might mean taking short naps during the day, especially if you've had a particularly active or stressful period. It could also involve scheduling regular breaks during work or household tasks to avoid overexerting yourself and exacerbating pain and fatigue.

During these rest periods, focus on engaging in relaxing, low-energy activities that bring you joy and help you unwind. This might include reading, listening to music, practicing gentle stretches, or simply sitting quietly and focusing on your breath.

Remember, rest and sleep are not luxuries, but essential components of a comprehensive arthritis management plan. By prioritizing adequate rest and taking steps to improve your sleep quality, you'll be better equipped to manage your symptoms, reduce inflammation, and maintain a high quality of life despite the challenges of living with arthritis.

If you continue to struggle with sleep disturbances or excessive fatigue despite implementing these strategies, don't hesitate to consult with your healthcare provider. They can help identify any underlying issues and develop a personalized plan to improve your rest and sleep quality.

Chapter 17: Frequently Asked Questions

Q: Can an anti-inflammatory diet really help with my arthritis pain?

Dr. Wells: Absolutely! I've seen numerous patients experience significant reductions in pain and inflammation after adopting an anti-inflammatory diet. One memorable case was a 62-year-old woman named Sarah who had been living with severe rheumatoid arthritis for over a decade. After just three months of following the diet and making some key lifestyle changes, she reported a 50% reduction in her pain levels and a marked improvement in her mobility. The key is to be consistent and patient, as it can take time for the body to adjust and heal.

Q: Do I have to give up all my favorite foods to follow an anti-inflammatory diet?

Dr. Wells: Not necessarily. While an anti-inflammatory diet does involve limiting or avoiding certain foods that can trigger inflammation, such as processed snacks, refined sugars, and unhealthy fats, there are still plenty of delicious and satisfying options to enjoy. Focus on incorporating a variety of fresh, whole foods like fruits, vegetables, whole grains, lean proteins, and healthy fats. With a little creativity and experimentation, you'll discover new favorite meals that nourish your body without sacrificing taste.

Q: Is it expensive to eat an anti-inflammatory diet?

Dr. Wells: It can be, but it doesn't have to be. Some of the healthiest, most anti-inflammatory foods are actually quite affordable, such as seasonal produce, legumes, and whole grains. Planning your meals in advance, buying in bulk, and cooking at home can also help keep costs down. Remember, investing in your health now can save you money on medical expenses down the line.

Q: How long does it take to see results from an anti-inflammatory diet?

Dr. Wells: The timeline can vary from person to person, depending on factors like the severity of your arthritis, your overall health, and how consistently you follow the diet. Some people may notice improvements in their symptoms within a few weeks, while for others, it may take several months. I encourage my patients to stay committed to the process and celebrate even small victories along the way.

Q: Can I still eat out at restaurants while following an anti-inflammatory diet?

Dr. Wells: Yes, you can! Many restaurants now offer healthier options that align with an anti-inflammatory diet, such as salads, grilled fish or chicken, and vegetable-based dishes. Don't be afraid to ask questions about how meals are prepared and request modifications if needed, like asking for dressings or sauces on the side. With a little planning and assertiveness, you can still enjoy dining out with friends and family while staying on track with your diet.

Q: Are there any supplements that can help enhance the effects of an anti-inflammatory diet?

Dr. Wells: While a nutritious, well-rounded diet should always be the foundation of your arthritis management plan, certain supplements may provide additional benefits. Omega-3 fatty acids, found in fish oil supplements, have been shown to help reduce inflammation and improve joint health. Curcumin, the active compound in turmeric, has also demonstrated anti-inflammatory properties. However, it's crucial to consult with your healthcare provider before starting any new supplement regimen to ensure safety and avoid potential interactions with medications.

Q: I have a sweet tooth. Are there any anti-inflammatory desserts I can enjoy?

Dr. Wells: Absolutely! While processed sweets laden with refined sugars can contribute to inflammation, there are plenty of delicious and nutritious dessert options that can satisfy your cravings without sabotaging your progress. Some of my favorites include fresh fruit sorbet, chia seed pudding sweetened with a touch of raw honey, and dark chocolate-dipped strawberries. The key is to focus on whole, natural ingredients and enjoy treats in moderation.

Q: Can I still enjoy alcoholic beverages while following an anti-inflammatory diet?

Dr. Wells: While it's best to limit alcohol consumption when managing arthritis, enjoying a drink occasionally is generally okay. Red wine, in particular, contains antioxidants like resveratrol that may help reduce inflammation. However, it's important to drink in moderation, as excessive alcohol intake can actually increase inflammation and interfere with the effectiveness of certain medications. As a general rule, I advise my patients to stick to no more than one drink per day for women and two drinks per day for men.

Q: I'm a vegetarian. Can I still follow an anti-inflammatory diet?

Dr. Wells: Yes, you can! An anti-inflammatory diet can be adapted to suit a variety of dietary preferences, including vegetarianism. Focus on incorporating plenty of anti-inflammatory plant-based foods into your meals, such as leafy greens, colorful fruits and vegetables, whole grains, legumes, nuts, and seeds. If you eat eggs and dairy, opt for organic, free-range eggs and low-fat, unsweetened dairy products. With a little planning and creativity, you can create a well-rounded, anti-inflammatory diet that meets your nutritional needs as a vegetarian.

Q: How important is staying hydrated when managing arthritis symptoms?

Dr. Wells: Staying well-hydrated is crucial for overall health and can be particularly beneficial for people with arthritis. Adequate hydration helps lubricate your joints, reduce inflammation, and flush out toxins from your body. Aim to drink at least 8-10 glasses of water per day, and more if you're exercising or spending time in hot weather. If plain water feels boring, try infusing it with fresh fruits, herbs, or cucumber slices for a refreshing twist.

Q: Can I still enjoy coffee on an anti-inflammatory diet?

Dr. Wells: Yes, you can still enjoy coffee in moderation on an anti-inflammatory diet. In fact, some studies suggest that coffee may even have anti-inflammatory properties, thanks to its high antioxidant content. However, it's important to be mindful of what you add to your coffee. Avoid loading up on sugar, artificial sweeteners, and high-fat creamers, which can negate the potential benefits. Instead, try using unsweetened plant-based milks like almond or coconut milk, and sweeten with a touch of raw honey or cinnamon if desired.

Q: Are there any foods that can help alleviate morning stiffness?

Dr. Wells: Yes, certain foods can help reduce inflammation and alleviate morning stiffness. One of my top recommendations is to incorporate tart cherries into your diet, either fresh, frozen, or in the form of unsweetened tart cherry juice. Tart cherries are packed with antioxidants and have been shown to help reduce inflammation and ease joint pain. Another helpful strategy is to start your day with a warm, anti-inflammatory beverage like ginger tea or the turmeric latte I mentioned earlier. The warmth can help soothe stiff joints, while the anti-inflammatory compounds in these spices get to work from the inside out.

Q: How can I make meal planning and preparation easier while following an anti-inflammatory diet?

Dr. Wells: Meal planning and preparation can feel overwhelming at first, but with a little practice and organization, it can become a simple and enjoyable part of your routine. One strategy I recommend is to dedicate a few hours on the weekend to prep ingredients for the week ahead, like chopping vegetables, cooking whole grains, and marinating proteins. Having these components ready to go can make assembling meals throughout the week a breeze. Another helpful tip is to make double batches of your favorite anti-inflammatory recipes and freeze half for later, so you always have a healthy meal on hand when life gets busy. Remember, the key is to find a system that works for you and your lifestyle.

Conclusion & Free Resources

Dear Reader,

As we come to the end of this book, I want to express my heartfelt gratitude for your trust and dedication in embarking on this transformative journey towards better health and well-being. By choosing to adopt an anti-inflammatory diet and lifestyle, you have taken a significant step towards managing your arthritis symptoms and improving your overall quality of life.

Throughout these pages, we have explored the science behind inflammation, the role of nutrition in managing arthritis, and practical strategies for making sustainable lifestyle changes. I hope that the information, recipes, and meal plans provided have empowered you to take control of your health and given you the tools needed to create lasting, positive changes.

Your journey towards optimal health does not end here.

To further support you in your efforts, I am excited to offer a range of additional resources that can be accessed by scanning the QR code below.

These complimentary materials include:

- **Printable Anti-Inflammatory Food Pyramid:** A visual guide to help you make informed food choices and prioritize anti-inflammatory ingredients in your diet.
- **Arthritis-Friendly Exercise Guide:** A collection of safe and effective exercises designed to improve flexibility, strengthen muscles, and reduce joint pain and stiffness.
- **Anti-Inflammatory Ingredient Substitution Chart:** A handy reference tool to help you easily swap out pro-inflammatory ingredients for healthier, anti-inflammatory alternatives in your favorite recipes.

By taking advantage of these bonus resources, you will be even better equipped to integrate the principles of an anti-inflammatory lifestyle into your daily routines and continue making progress on your health journey.

Thank you again for your trust and for allowing me to be a part of your journey. I wish you all the best in your ongoing pursuit of optimal health and well-being.

With gratitude,

Dr. Madison Wells

Made in the USA
Middletown, DE
20 December 2024

67609986R00062